The Complete Hamilton Beach Dual Breakfast Sandwich Maker Cookbook: Simple Quick And Delicious for Busy Beginners

The Hamilton Beach Double breakfast sandwich maker is sure to exceed your expectations. It allows you to make two sandwiches at the same time, double the efficiency and half the time! This book will give you an in-depth look at the benefits it can bring to your cooking. Especially for those with busy schedules, it offers many quick recipes that are not only easy but also extremely delicious. We sincerely hope that you will enjoy this cookbook and make the most of it in your culinary journey.

Tony Blackwell

Table of Contents

★ Chapter 1:Basic Knowledge

Introduction 01
What's a Hamilton Beach breakfast sandwich maker? 03
About the features of Hamilton Beach breakfast sandwich makers? 04
The Outstanding Advantages of the Hamilton Beach Breakfast Sandwich Maker. ... 05
Tips and Precautions for breakfast sandwich machine use 06
Multiple ways to make breakfast sandwiches 07
Troubleshooting Guide for Hamilton Beach Breakfast Sandwich Machin 08

★ Chapter 2:Classic breakfast sandwich

Ham and Cheese Sandwich 10
Bacon and Egg Sandwich 10
Hash Brown Sausage Sandwich 11
Tomato Basil Flatbread 11
Mustardy Egg Muffin Melt 12
Classic Bacon,Lettuce, and Tomato Sandwich 12
Egg and Cheese Sandwich 13
Mayo Avocado,and Cucumber Sandwich 13
Mexican Fried Egg Sandwich 14
Egg,Avocado, and Bacon Sandwich 15
Egg and Ham Sandwich 15
Steak & Eggs Sandwich 16
Almond Pancake With Egg And Prosciutto 16
Pesto Cheese Sandwich 17
Pancake, Sausage & Egg Sandwich 17
Sausage Muffin Sandwich 18
Creamy Scrambled Egg Sandwich 18
Egg-and-Cheese Muffins 19
Egg, Spinach, and Parmesan Sandwich 20
Ham and Cheddar Muffin 20
Eggs-in-a-Hole Sandwich with Bacon 21
Ham and cheese sandwich 21

★ Chapter 3:Poultry Breakfast Sandwiches and Burgers

Grilled Chicken and Avocado Sandwich 23
Chicken Pesto Sandwich 23
Chicken And Bacon Paprika Sandwich 24
Spinach And Pesto Chicken Panini 24
Cheesy Chicken Waffle Sandwich 25
Lemony Chicken and Cheery Sandwich 25
The Ultimate Chicken, Spinach And Mozzarella Sandwich ... 26
Bacon Chipotle Chicken Panini 26
Bruschetta Turkey Panini 27
Chicken burger 27

Mushroom, Turkey, and Swiss Cheese Burgers ———— 28
Herbed Chicken and Onion Burger ———— 29
Turkey Burgers with Honey and Mustard ———— 29
Chicken and Avocado Pita Sandwich ———— 30
Mayo Chicken Salad Sandwich ———— 31
Chicken Cordon Bleu Sandwich ———— 31
Basil Chicken Burger with Pizza Sauce ———— 32
Mayo Turkey Burger ———— 32
Turkey Burger with Tzatziki Sauce ———— 33

⭐ Chapter 4: Beef And Pork Breakfast Sandwich Recipes

Beef And Veggies Bagel Sandwich ———— 35
Mayo Roasted Beef Muffin Sandwiches ———— 35
Pesto Beef And Mozzarella Panini ———— 36
Authentic Philly Steak Sandwich ———— 36
Bolognese Cup ———— 37
Beef, Waffle, And Egg Sandwich ———— 38
The Ultimate 4-minute Cheeseburger ———— 38
Spicy Beef Muffin Delight ———— 39
Spicy Horseradish Beef And Cheese Panini ———— 39
Cored Beef And Cabbage Panini ———— 40
Cheesy Beef And Egg Sandwich ———— 40
Worcestershire Beef and Cheddar Sandwich ———— 41
Coleslaw and Comned Beef Sandwich ———— 42
Classic Beef Cheese Burger ———— 42
Garlic Beef Sandwiches ———— 43
Spicy Beef Burger ———— 44
Mushroom Beef Burger ———— 44
Pulled Pork Sandwich ———— 45
Roasted Beef and Provolone Muffin Sandwich ———— 45
Herbed Beef and Giardiniera Sandwich ———— 46
Beef and Fried Mushroom Sandwich ———— 47
Beef and Carrot Sandwich ———— 48
Pork And Egg Tortilla Open Sandwich ———— 48
Hot Pork Sausage And Scrambled Egg Sandwich ———— 49
Pork Muffin Sandwich ———— 49
Veggie And Pork Mayo Sandwich ———— 50
Spicy Pork And Pimento Sandwich ———— 50
Mayo Gourmet Pork Sandwich ———— 51
Herbed Cauliflower and Pork Sandwich ———— 51
Apple and Pork Muffin Mell ———— 52
Pan-fried pork sandwich ———— 53

⭐ Chapter 5: Fish and Seafood Recipes

Salmon and Pistachio sandwich ———— 54

Awesome Salmon Burgers with Harissa Mayo ······· 54
Crab Cake and Biscuit Sandwich ······· 55
Tuna and Com Muffin Sandwich ······· 56
Nutritious Salmon Bacon Sandwich ······· 56
Snapper cheese energy sandwich ······· 57
Nutritious fish finger vitality meal ······· 57
Tender cod pita sandwich ······· 58
Delicious shrimp biscuit sandwich ······· 58
Vibrant shrimp Pan burger ······· 59
Relishing Salmon and Bacon Sandwic ······· 59
Fish Finger Sandwich ······· 60
Tilapia And Pimento Dijon Sandwich ······· 60
Salmon And Pistachio Melt ······· 61
Cod and Slaw Sandwiches with Tartar Sauce ······· 61
Mexican-style Seafood Burger ······· 62
Mayo Shrimp Sandwich ······· 63
Lobster Rolls with Basil ······· 63
Mayo Scallop Com Burgers ······· 64
Lemony Shrimp Cod Burgers ······· 65
Mayo Shrimp Salad Burgers ······· 65

★ Chapter 6:Fruit Breakfast Sandwich Recipes

Fruit Salad Sandwich With Lemon ······· 67
Cinnamon Raisin Apple Sandwich ······· 67
Caramel Strawberries Sandwich ······· 68
Honey Blueberry and Pear Croissant ······· 68
Apple Sandwich with Strawberry Jam ······· 69
Honey Nut Mix Sandwich ······· 69
Sweet Mango-Peach Sandwich ······· 70
Cheddar-apple Smoked Bacon Sandwich ······· 70
Gruyere, Apple And Ham Sandwich ······· 71
Blueberry Waffle Sandwich ······· 71
Apple And Brie Croissant Sandwich ······· 72
Pineapple and Coconut Filled Croissant Sandwich ······· 72
Berry Pancake ······· 73
Spicy Cream Cheese Raspberry Croissant ······· 73
Maple Apple Sandwich ······· 74
Peanut Butter Banana Sandwich ······· 74
Dark Chocolate Sandwich with Cherries ······· 75
Peach Bran Sandwich ······· 75
Apple, Pineapple, and Banana Sandwich ······· 76
Japanese Fruit Sandwich with Strawberries, Kiwis, and Oranges ······· 76

★ Chapter 7:Vegetarian Breakfast Recipes

Eggplant Sandwich ······· 78
Tomato Basil Flatbread ······· 78
Beans & Veggies Sandwich ······· 79
Spinach Havarti Sandwich ······· 79
Vegetarian Boca Sandwich ······· 80

Avocado And Mixed Vegetable Panini ···································· 80
Sauerkraut Sandwich ··· 81
Veggie & Cheese Melt ·· 81
Lemony Delicious Summer Vegetable Panini ························ 82
Veggie Burgers ·· 82
Com Bowl With Tomato, Bacon,And Cheese ························ 83
Easy Ham And Scrambled Egg ······································· 84
Portabella And Spinach Croissant ·································· 84
Garlic Black Bean and Tomato Burgers ····························· 85
Avocado and Mushroom Burger ···································· 85
Avocado,Cucumber, and Broccoli Sandwich ······················ 86
Garlic Buffalo Chickpeas Burgers ·································· 87
Florentine Biscuit with Yogurt ····································· 87
Egg and Cheese Seed Bagel ··· 88
Egg Whites and Cheese on Ciabatta ································· 88

★ Chapter 8:Gluten-Free Sandwiches Recipes

Mexican Gluten-free Pork Sandwich ······························· 90
Almond Pancake with Egg and Prosciutto ························· 90
Gluten Free Smoked Salmon and Cream Cheese Sandwich ········ 91
Avocado Sandwich with Egg,Ham and Cheese ····················· 91
Combread and Egg Sandwich ······································· 92
Almond Flour Waffle and Sausage Sandwich ······················ 92
Com Bowl with Tomato,Bacon,and Cheese ························ 93
Gluten-Free Crispy Grilled Cheese and Bacon Sandwich ·········· 93

★ Chapter 9:Keto Sandwich Recipes

Mushrooms and Crab Melt Sandwich ······························· 95
Cheddar and Cauliflower Sandwich ································· 95
Avocado Chicken Sandwich ··· 96
Herbed Cauliflower and Pork Sandwich ···························· 97
Mayo Beef Sandwich ·· 97
Avocado and Cauliflower Bagel Sandwiches ······················ 98
Hearty Scrambled Egg Sandwich ···································· 99
Tofu, Ham, and Cheese Sandwich ··································· 99
Cuban Bacon and Tomato Sandwich ······························· 100
Keto Chicken, Cauliflower,and Cranberry Sandwich ·············· 101
Egg, Watercress,and Beef Sandwich ······························· 101
Chicken and Avocado Panini ·· 102
Spinach,Avocado,and Cheese Panini ······························ 103
Mushroom-Cucumber Panini ······································· 103
Keto Sausage and Cheddar Sandwich ······························ 104
Keto Com Blue Com Pork Sandwich ································· 104

★ Chapter 10:Snacks and Desserts Sandwich Recipes

Chocolate Donut Dessert Sandwich ································· 106

The Ultimate 4-minute Cheeseburger ···················· 106
Herbed Omelet With Cream Cheese And Cheddar ········ 107
Chocolate Chip Waffle Sandwich ······················· 107
Caramel Cashew Waffle Sandwich ····················· 108
Olive And Cheese Snack ······························· 108
English Muffin Sandwich ······························· 109
Vanilla Mini Cake ···································· 109
Pizza Sandwich ···································· 109
Orange Dream Donut ································ 110
Strawberry and Hazelnut Bagel Sandwich ·············· 110
Blueberry Marshmallow Sandwich ····················· 111
Chocolate Banana Croissant ·························· 111
Ham, Apple, and Cheese Panini ······················· 112
Honey Apple Pie Panini ······························· 112
Nutella Banana Panini ································ 113
Cinnamon Strawberry English Muffin Pies ·············· 114
Nut Butter Banana Chocolate Chip Panini ·············· 114
Brie Strawberry Cheese Muffin Sandwich ··············· 115
Lemony Raspberry English Muffin Pies ················· 115

 Conclusion ···················· 117

Quick and easy and ready to eat in 5 minutes

Introduction

The Ultimate Hamilton Beach Dual Breakfast Sandwich Maker Cookbook is a cookbook focused on the Hamilton Beach Dual breakfast sandwich maker. This book details the many features and advantages of the sandwich machine, and aims to help readers better understand and use this kitchen appliance.

The Hamilton Beach Breakfast Sandwich Maker is a portable and convenient kitchen appliance that prepares delicious and healthy breakfasts for you and your family. Simply add egg whites, spinach, green peppers, tomato slices and cheese to a cooking dish and it quickly makes a nutritious breakfast. Made of non-stick materials and energy-efficient cooking equipment, the machine features two pilot lights (red and green), two heating plates with handles, detachable ring assemblies and a lid. It can make not only sandwiches, but also tortillas, cookies, toast, bagels and many other foods, and is a desktop cooking appliance suitable for any time indoors.

The sandwich maker is very simple to set up, its parts are removable, dishwasher safe and durable. It has many benefits, such as being able to make sandwiches in less than five minutes, the cleaning process is simple, and you can use it to make a variety of different sandwiches. Whether it's bread, bagels, waffles, tortillas, pancakes or cookies, you can use them to make sandwiches. In order to make a healthy and delicious sandwich, it is recommended to use fresh ingredients.

The Hamilton Beach Double Breakfast Sandwich Maker is made up of simple parts and functions to make every type of sandwich. If you are on a ketogenic diet, make meat sandwiches; If you are a vegetarian, you can make vegetarian sandwiches. With this appliance, you can make a healthy breakfast sandwich, as well as a lunch, dinner or snack sandwich. It prepares sandwiches in 5 minutes or less, saving time and money.

With many kitchen appliances appearing on the market in recent years, from multi-functional cookware to air fryers, technology has really changed the way people prepare and cook food, making it faster and more convenient to accommodate the more hectic and fast-paced lifestyles of today's society. It can feel overwhelming to find the right kitchen appliance to invest in among the many options. If you love sandwiches, or often prepare them for your family, investing in a sandwich maker is a really good idea, not only to save time, but also to reduce your workload and free you up for other important things.

The Hamilton Beach Double Breakfast Sandwich Maker will undoubtedly exceed your expectations by helping you prepare two sandwiches at once, doubling your efficiency and halving your time! Through this book, you will gain a deeper understanding of the convenience this wonderful kitchen appliance can bring to your cooking. Many quick and delicious recipes have also been added, and I hope you will enjoy this cookbook.

What's a Hamilton Beach breakfast sandwich maker?

The Hamilton Beach Breakfast Sandwich Maker is a satisfying kitchen appliance that makes sandwiches in five minutes or less. Designed to resemble an English muffin, it is simple to assemble and can be used to create a restaurant-style sandwich.

Breakfast is considered the most important meal of the day, but for many people, especially families with young children, mornings are often hectic. The Hamilton Beach Breakfast Sandwich Maker solves this problem by allowing you to make fresh breakfast sandwiches that are easy to carry around. Simply choose your favorite bread, add your favorite toppings such as cheese, pre-cooked meat or other ingredients, and enjoy the perfect breakfast sandwich in four minutes. You can also personalize your sandwich with a variety of fresh ingredients.

It's important to note that the Hamilton Beach Breakfast Sandwich Maker is not a high-tech, fancy cooking tool designed for professional chefs, but rather a fun, practical, sturdy appliance that makes it easy to create a fast food-like breakfast sandwich that is suitable for everyone, even those who don't know much about cooking.

The idea is to create a breakfast sandwich similar to a fast food restaurant, but using fresh and healthy ingredients. The assembly process is simple: start at the bottom of the muffin, add meat, cheese or vegetables, close the section, place an egg in the next layer, and then top the egg with slices of bread. Close the lid, and in about five minutes, the eggs are cooked, the bread is baked, and a delicious sandwich is ready. Simply slide out from under the egg and the whole sandwich is ready to enjoy.

The machine is equipped with a lid, cooking plate, bottom heating plate, pilot light (green and red), cooking plate handle, detachable ring assembly, top heating plate and base. The green light is used for preheating, and the red light is the power button for turning the machine on and off.

When using for the first time, remove the cap and remove the ring assembly, rinse in the dishwasher or with warm soapy water and wipe dry. Wipe the upper and lower heating plates with a damp cloth of soapy water, then remove the soap with a damp cloth and dry thoroughly. Spray the ring with nonstick cooking spray or brush with vegetable oil.

In conclusion, the Hamilton Beach Breakfast Sandwich Maker is a great choice for the kitchen, offering a convenient and efficient way to make breakfast sandwiches to start your day off with a nutritious and delicious breakfast. Whether it's a busy parent, student or anyone who wants a quick and easy breakfast, this appliance has you covered. So, don't let the morning pass without a Hamilton Beach breakfast sandwich maker, give it a try and experience the convenience and taste it brings!

About the features of Hamilton Beach breakfast sandwich makers?

Quick and easy: Sandwiches can be made in five minutes or less to save time in the morning.

Reasonable design:
Appearance: Designed to resemble an English muffin shape.
Components: Fitted with lid, cooking plate, bottom heating plate, pilot light (green and red), cooking plate handle, detachable ring assembly, top heating plate and base.

Function: Green indicator for preheating and red indicator for power button for turning off/on sandwich maker.

Easy assembly: The assembly process is simple and can be easily operated by anyone.

Personalization: The sandwich can be customized according to personal taste using a variety of fresh ingredients such as bread, meat, cheese, vegetables and seasonings.

Easy to clean: The removable ring assembly can be washed in the dishwasher, and the bottom and top heating plates can be wiped with a soapy water soft sponge for easy cleaning.

Wide range of applications: not only can you make breakfast sandwiches, but you can also prepare lunch, dinner or snack sandwiches.

Freezing function: The breakfast sandwich can be frozen very well, easy to enjoy at any time.

The Outstanding Advantages of the Hamilton Beach Breakfast Sandwich Maker.

In today's fast-paced world, having a reliable and efficient kitchen appliance can make a significant difference, especially when it comes to breakfast. The Hamilton Beach Breakfast Sandwich Maker offers several remarkable benefits that can transform your morning routine.

Quick and Convenient Breakfast Preparation

Time is of the essence in the morning, and this sandwich maker understands that. You can whip up a scrumptious breakfast in under five minutes. Just gather your favorite ingredients - be it fresh bread, succulent tomatoes, fluffy eggs, or gooey cheese - assemble them on the cooking plate, and let the magic happen. No more rushing around or skipping breakfast due to time constraints. For instance, imagine starting your day with a perfectly toasted sandwich filled with crispy bacon and melted cheddar in just a few minutes.

Simple Cleaning Process

Cleaning up after cooking is a breeze with the Hamilton Beach Breakfast Sandwich Maker. All its components are detachable, allowing for effortless removal and easy cleaning. You can either pop them into the dishwasher or give them a quick wash with soapy water. This saves you precious time and ensures your kitchen remains tidy. Say goodbye to the hassle of scrubbing stubborn stains.

Versatile One-Dish Meals

This appliance isn't limited to just making traditional sandwiches. It gives you the freedom to create a wide range of one-dish meals. From assembling classic tomato and egg sandwiches to experimenting with unique combinations like bagels with smoked salmon or tortillas filled with spicy chicken, the possibilities are endless.

Innovative Breakfast Options

With the Hamilton Beach Breakfast Sandwich Maker, you can break away from the monotony of the same old breakfast. It enables you to prepare an array of delightful treats such as pancake sandwiches, savory muffins, or even fluffy omelets. Customize your breakfast to suit your taste buds and mood each day.

User-Friendly Design

Designed with the user in mind, this appliance is incredibly easy to operate. Whether you're cooking for a small family or a larger group, you can prepare multiple batches of breakfast quickly and effortlessly. No need for complicated instructions or hours of standing in the kitchen. Just plug it in, and you're on your way to a delicious start of the day.

In conclusion, the Hamilton Beach Breakfast Sandwich Maker is not just an appliance; it's a game-changer for your breakfast experience. Say hello to quick, easy, and delicious mornings!

Tips and Precautions for breakfast sandwich machine use

Here are some things you need to know before using a breakfast sandwich maker

- First of all, be sure to read the complete instruction manual carefully to ensure that you can operate the equipment correctly.
- For ideal results, prioritize rolls, bagels, or plain bread for your sandwich.
- Prepare the necessary ingredients in advance before cooking the sandwich, which will make the process smoother for you.
- When the unit is preheating, make sure the lid is closed and the seals and cooking plates are in place.
- Check the state of the cooking plate before adding sandwich ingredients during preheating.
- Children should not be allowed to play with this device as a toy.
- Do not touch the hot surface of the breakfast sandwich maker to prevent burns.
- Wear insulated gloves and use the handle to lift the cooking plate.
- Unplug from wall outlet and allow to cool before not using or cleaning.
- Never immerse the cooking unit in water or any other liquid.
- This is an appliance for indoor use, not for outdoor use.
- Do not place the device on or near a heating element.
- Do not use sharp instruments to remove food.

- Wait for food to cool before cleaning.
- Adjust the cooking time of the breakfast sandwich maker according to the actual situation.
- Gently lower the lid without pressing hard.
- Press the red light to turn the breakfast sandwich maker on or off.
- Do not move the breakfast sandwich maker during use.
- If you are using larger sized waffles or toast, you can cut them with cookie molds.
- When using meat, seafood or vegetables, they should be cooked in advance before being placed in the sandwich maker.
- Clean pantry, utensils, and countertops before use.
- Follow the recipe instructions to accurately measure the amount of ingredients.
- Read the recipe twice before preparing breakfast.
- Before enjoying, taste the breakfast.
- Buy fresh vegetables, meat, cheese and eggs.
- Do not use oversized eggs, or the egg may leak out of the device.
- Do not overfill the cooking plate.
- If the food is not cooked properly, you can increase the cooking time appropriately. For frozen ingredients, it is best to thaw them at room temperature before placing them in the breakfast sandwich maker.
- It is generally appropriate to adjust the cooking time to five minutes.

Multiple ways to make breakfast sandwiches

There are so many different ways to make a great breakfast sandwich. Here are some useful and popular sandwich types and ingredients to pair them with:

Sandwich Type :
   For example, you can try a cheese bagel sandwich, a sausage and biscuit sandwich, a cheese and egg sandwich or a bacon sandwich.

Bread Selection :
   Choose from English muffins, bagels, blueberry bread, cranberry bread, banana bread, waffles, pancakes, cookies, sandwich flakes, croissants and more to provide a diverse base for your sandwich.

Meat Ingredients :
   If you prefer meat sandwiches, choose pre-cooked bacon, beef, chicken, Turkey, fish, sausage, ham, Turkey bacon, Canadian bacon, vegetarian meat substitutes, etc., to meet your different tastes and nutritional needs.

Cheese Type :

Cheese is one of the key ingredients when making sandwiches. Cheddar cheese, mozzarella cheese, Swiss cheese, American cheese, blue cheese, feta cheese, etc. are all good choices. You can use your favorite cheese in different sandwiches according to your personal preference.

Vegetables :

To make the sandwich more delicious, try adding vegetables such as apple slices, spinach, avocado, peppers, tomatoes or shallots. You can freely choose your favorite green ingredients to add flavor and nutrition.

Seasoning added :

You can add mayonnaise, ketchup, peppermint chutney or any other condiment you like to make the sandwich more appealing.

Use of eggs :

Use egg whites, yolks or scrambled eggs to enrich the texture and nutrition of the sandwich.

More Uses for sandwiches ;

Don't limit yourself to making breakfast sandwiches, you can also use the Hamilton Beach Breakfast Sandwich Maker to prepare lunch, dinner or snack sandwiches.

Frozen Preservation of sandwiches :

Breakfast sandwiches freeze well. Prepare sandwiches for the weekend ahead of time and have a great weekend with your family. Turn frozen sandwiches into delicious treats.

For best freezing results: Let the sandwich cool at room temperature first, then wrap it in plastic wrapping paper. Put it in a bag and store it in the freezer.

When a quick breakfast is needed, open the freezer and remove the bag. Remove one or more sandwiches from the bag. Wrap in paper towels and defrost in the oven for half a minute to a minute. Then, heat on high for 1 minute.

Troubleshooting Guide for Hamilton Beach Breakfast Sandwich Machine

In the process of using the Hamilton Beach breakfast sandwich machine, you may encounter some problems, especially if it is not used and maintained properly. The following are common problems and solutions:

Poor heating, slow or low temperature :

Green indicator used to preheat the device. When the light turns green, it means the device is warming up to the exact temperature, but it doesn't mean the sandwich is ready. You should follow the cooking time specified in the recipe. The green light usually comes on in 5 to 7 minutes, and most sandwiches are ready within 5 minutes. If the green light comes on after 3 minutes, you should wait another 1 minute before opening the lid of the breakfast sandwich maker and removing the sandwich.

If you want to make another batch using the sandwich mechanism, wait 2 minutes before putting in the sandwich to give the device enough time to reach the exact temperature.

When there are too many ingredients on the cooking plate, it may cause uneven heating. So, reduce the amount of ingredients on the cooking board. And make sure that the cover of the device is closed and the cooking plate and seal are in the correct position when preheating.

Eggs overcooked :

The cooking time to make the sandwich is about 5 minutes, and the eggs can be overcooked. You may not be able to undo this in this operation, but you can learn from this mistake. In later preparation, reduce cooking time. Please note that cooking times may vary for very small eggs, scrambled eggs, or egg whites.

Eggs undercooked and bread underbaked :

This may be due to the use of frozen or extra large eggs. This means that you need to increase the cooking time for the sandwich maker. For frozen ingredients, you can thaw them at room temperature first and then add the ingredients to the cooking plate, otherwise it will affect the cooking time of the sandwich maker.

Egg leaking from seal ring :

This can be caused by too many ingredients on the cooking board. Do not use extra large eggs. Use medium eggs for sandwiches. Also reduce the amount of other ingredients in the sandwich and do not press the lid. Also make sure that the cooking plate is positioned accurately, that the equipment is fully heated, and that fresh egg whites are used to make the sandwiches.

Ingredients stick to sealing ring or non-stick cooking plate :

Use a plastic or wooden spatula or utensil to loosen the ingredients when they stick to the seal or non-stick cooking plate. But before using the sandwich maker, you should lightly spray the seal or cooking plate with nonstick cooking spray.

Toast burnt :

Sugar and high fat content can cause the bread to be darker. You can cook the eggs without the bread and lid first. When the cooking time is almost over, add the bread to the sandwich machine. This way you can quickly make delicious and healthy sandwiches for your family, no trouble.

The lid goes up while cooking the sandwich :

This can be caused by a lot of air being stirred into the eggs when they are cooked. Do not press the lid.

HAM AND CHEESE SANDWICH

 PREPARATION TIME: 10 MINUTES

 COOKING TIME: 5 MINUTES

 SERVINGS: 1

INGREDIENTS

- 2 slices of ham
- 1 slice of cheese
- 1 egg
- 2 slices of bread
- 1 leaf of lettuce

PREPARATION:

1. Preheat your Hamilton Beach Breakfast Sandwich Maker.

2. Lift the top cover, ring, and cooking plate.

3. Crack the egg on the bottom baking plate and close the lid to fry it until cooked.

4. Place a slice of bread, lay the lettuce leaf, ham slices and cheese slice on it.

5. Put the fried egg on top and cover with the other slice of bread.

6. Fasten the breakfast machine and wait for a few minutes until the sandwich is golden brown.

7. When finished cooking, rotate the handle of the cooking plate clockwise until it stops.

8. Lift the hood, the rings and transfer the sandwich to a plate.

★ Serving Suggestion: Serve with a cup of milk.

★ Variation Tip:Use different types of cheese for a change.

 **NUTRITION FACTS:**

Calories: 450 | Fat: 18g | Sodium: 650mg | Carbs: 40g | Fiber: 5g | Sugar: 8g | Protein: 30g

BACON AND EGG SANDWICH

 PREPARATION TIME: 8 MINUTES

 COOKING TIME: 6 MINUTES

 SERVINGS: 1

INGREDIENTS

- 2 slices of bacon
- 1 egg
- 1 slice of cheese
- 2 slices of bread

PREPARATION:

1. Preheat your Hamilton Beach Breakfast Sandwich Maker.

2. Lift the top cover, ring, and cooking plate.

3. Put the bacon in and fry until slightly crispy.

4. Crack the egg and fry it until cooked.

5. Place a slice of bread, then stack the cheese slice, bacon and egg in sequence.

6. Cover with the other slice of bread.

7. Close the breakfast machine and heat until the sandwich takes shape.

8. When finished cooking, rotate the handle of the cooking plate clockwise until it stops.

9. Lift the hood, the rings and transfer the sandwich to a plate.

10. Serve.

 **NUTRITION FACTS:**

Calories 300 | Fat 15g |Sodium 700mg | Carbs 22g | Fiber 2.5g | Sugar 5g | Protein 18g

HASH BROWN SAUSAGE SANDWICH

PREPARATION TIME: 8 MINUTES   COOKING TIME: 5 MINUTES   SERVINGS: 1

INGREDIENTS

- 2 frozen hash brown patties
- 1 turkey sausage patty
- 1 slice cheddar cheese
- 1 large egg, beaten

PREPARATION:

1. Heat the butter in a small skillet over medium heat. Add the hash brown patties and cook until lightly browned on one side.

2. Flip the patties and cook until browned on the other side

3. Preheat the breakfast sandwich maker.

4. Place one of the hash brown patties inside the bottom ring of the sandwich maker.

5. Top the hash brown with the sausage patty and slice of cheddar cheese.

6. Slide the egg tray into place and crack the egg into it.

7. Top the egg with the other hash brown patty.

8. Close the sandwich maker and cook for 4 to 5 minutes until the egg is cooked through.

9. Carefully rotate the egg tray out of the sandwich maker then open the sandwich maker and enjoy your sandwich.

 **NUTRITION FACTS:**

Calories 450 | Fat 25g |Sodium 800mg | Carbs 30g | Fiber 2g | Sugar 3g | Protein 20g

TOMATO BASIL FLATBREAD

PREPARATION TIME: 5 MINUTES   COOKING TIME: 5 MINUTES   SERVINGS: 1

INGREDIENTS

- 1 small round flatbread
- 1 tsp. olive oil
- Salt and pepper to taste
- 1 thick slice ripe tomato
- 4 fresh basil leaves
- 1 slice fresh mozzarella cheese
- 1 large egg

PREPARATION:

1. Preheat the breakfast sandwich maker.

2. Place the round flatbread inside the bottom tray of the sandwich maker.

3. Brush the flatbread with the olive oil and sprinkle with salt and pepper.

4. Top the flatbread with the slice of tomato, basil leaves and mozzarella cheese.

5. Slide the egg tray into place and crack the egg into it. Use a fork to stir the egg, just breaking the yolk. Close the sandwich maker and cook for 4 to 5 minutes until the egg is cooked through

6. Carefully rotate the egg tray out of the sandwich maker then open the sandwich maker to enjoy your sandwich.

★ Serving Suggestion: Serve with a slice of orange.
★ Variation Tip: Use different types of herbs for a unique flavor.

NUTRITION FACTS:

Calories 300 | Fat 15g |Sodium 500mg | Carbs 20g | Fiber 2g | Sugar 3g | Protein 15g

MUSTARDY EGG MUFFIN MELT

PREPARATION TIME: 3 MINUTES | COOKING TIME: 4 MINUTES | SERVINGS: 1

INGREDIENTS

- 1 English Muffin
- 2 ounces shredded Cheddar Cheese
- 2 tsp Yellow Mustard
- 1 Egg
- Salt and Pepper, to taste
- 1 tsp chopped Parsley

PREPARATION:

1. Preheat and grease the sandwich maker with cooking spray.
2. Cut the English muffin in half and brush the insides with the mustard.
3. Whisk the egg and season it with salt and pepper. Stir in the chopped parsley.
4. When the green light appears, place half of the muffin in the bottom ring, with the cut-side down.
5. Top with the cheese.
6. Lower the top ring and cooking plate, and pour the whisked egg into the plate.

7. Top with the second muffin half, keeping the cut-side down.
8. Close and cook for 4 minutes.
9. Rotate clockwise and open.Transfer the sandwich to a plate and enjoy!

★ Serving Suggestion: Serve with a small salad.
★ Variation Tip: Use different types of cheeses for variety.

NUTRITION FACTS:

Calories 435 | Fat 25g |Sodium 700mg | Carbs 27g | Fiber 2.3g | Sugar 3g | Protein 26g

CLASSIC BACON, LETTUCE, AND TOMATO SANDWICH

PREPARATION TIME: 15 MINUTES | COOKING TIME: 5 MINUTES | SERVINGS: 1

INGREDIENTS

- 2 slices white bread, cut in 4-inch circle
- 3 bacon slices, cooked
- 2 thin tomato slices
- 1 leaf Romaine lettuce, torn in half
- 2 teaspoons mayonnaise

PREPARATION:

1. Preheat your Hamilton Beach Breakfast Sandwich Maker, the PREHEAT light gets green when it is heated to the correct temperature.
2. Lift the top cover, ring, and cooking plate.
3. Place one half of the bread in the sandwich maker.
4. Top it with mayonnaise, lettuce and tomato.

5. Now lower the cooking plate and top rings, then place the bacon on top.

6. Place the other top half of the bread on top.

7. Add the other circle of the bread on top.

8. Cover the top hood, and let the sandwich cook for 5 minutes.

9. When finished cooking, rotate the handle of the cooking plate clockwise until it stops.

10. Lift the hood, the rings and transfer the sandwich to a plate.

> ★ Serving Suggestion: Serve the sandwich with crispy bacon and your favorite sauce on the side.
> ★ Variation Tip: Add some additional ground black pepper to the filling.

NUTRITION FACTS:

Calories 267 | Fat 12g |Sodium 165mg | Carbs 39g | Fiber 1.4g | Sugar 22g | Protein 3.3g

EGG AND CHEESE SANDWICH

PREPARATION TIME: 15 MINUTES | COOKING TIME: 5 MINUTES | SERVINGS: 1

INGREDIENTS

- 1 English Muffin
- 1 large egg, beaten
- 1 cheese slice,
- Butter, or olive oil

PREPARATION:

1. Preheat your Hamilton Beach Breakfast Sandwich Maker.

2. Lift the top cover, ring, and cooking plate.

3. Place the lower half of the muffin in the sandwich maker.

---

4. Brush the top of the muffin half with butter.

5. Now lower the cooking plate and top rings then pour in the egg.

6. Top the egg with cheese slice and place the other top half of the muffin on top.

7. Cover the top hood, and let the sandwich cook for 5 minutes.

8. When finished cooking, rotate the handle of the cooking plate clockwise until it stop.Lift the hood, the rings and transfer the sandwich to a plate.

> ★ Serving Suggestion: Serve the sandwich with coleslaw and your favorite sauce on the side.
> ★ Variation Tip: Add some additional dried herbs to the filling.

NUTRITION FACTS:

Calories 273 | Fat 22g |Sodium 517mg | Carbs 3.3g | Fiber 0.2g | Sugar 1.4g | Protein 16.1g

MAYO AVOCADO, AND CUCUMBER SANDWICH

PREPARATION TIME: 15 MINUTES | COOKING TIME: 5 MINUTES | SERVINGS: 2

INGREDIENTS

- ¼ cup chives, chopped
- ¼ cup mayonnaise
- ¼ cup tarragon
- ¼ cup Greek yoghurt
- 1 lemon, halved
- 2 tablespoons olive oil
- Sat and black pepper, to taste
- ½ head of butter lettuce, leaves torn
- ¼ English cucumber, sliced
- 1 avocado, sliced

- 4 slices grainy bread, cut into 4 inches round
- 8 ounces mozzarella, sliced
- 2 cups alfalfa sprouts

PREPARATION:

1. Beat yoghurt with mayonnaise, tarragon, chives, black pepper and salt.

2. Preheat your Hamilton Beach Breakfast Sandwich Maker until PREHEAT light gets green.

3. Lift the top cover, ring, and cooking plate.

4. Place one bread slice inside the bottom tray of the sandwich maker.

5. Add ¼ lettuce, cucumber, avocado and the rest of the fillings.

6. Now lower the cooking plate and top rings.

7. Place another bread slice on top, then brush it with oil.

8. Cover the top hood, and let the sandwich cook for 5 minutes.

9. Rotate the handle of the cooking plate clockwise until it stops.Lift the hood, the rings and transfer the sandwich to a plate.Repeat the same steps with the remaining ingredients.

★ Serving Suggestion: Serve the sandwich with crispy zucchini fries on the side.
★ Variation Tip: You can add a lettuce leaves to the filling as well.

NUTRITION FACTS:

Calories 284 | Fat 7.9g |Sodium 704mg | Carbs 6g | Fiber 3.6g | Sugar 6g | Protein 18g

MEXICAN FRIED EGG SANDWICH

PREPARATION TIME: 15 MINUTES

COOKING TIME: 5 MINUTES

SERVINGS: 2

INGREDIENTS

- Mexican-style simple syrup
- ¾ cup Piloncillo sugar
- ½ cup water
- ½ cup whole cloves
- Peel of 1 orange
- 4 cinnamon sticks
- 1 raw almond, chopped

Sandwich:

- ¼ cup refried beans
- ½ teaspoon chilli powder
- 2 teaspoons olive oil
- 1 hamburger bun, split
- 1 fried egg
- ¼ sliced avocado
- 2 slices crispy bacon
- Hot sauce, for garnish
- Fresh cilantro, for garnish

PREPARATION:

1. Add sugar, water, whole cloves, orange peel, cinnamon sticks and almonds to a saucepan.

2. Cook for 10 minutes on low heat, then strain.

3. Preheat your Hamilton Beach Breakfast Sandwich Maker until PREHEAT light gets green.

4. Lift the top cover, ring, and cooking plate.

5. Place half of the English muffin, cut-side up, inside the bottom tray of the sandwich maker.

6. Spread the prepared syrup, refried beans and the rest of the ingredients on top.

7. Now lower the cooking plate and top rings.

8. Place the other top half of the muffin on top.

9. Cover the top hood, and let the sandwich cook for 5 minutes.

10. Rotate the handle of the cooking plate clockwise until it stops.

11. Lift the hood, the rings and transfer the sandwich to a plate.

NUTRITION FACTS:

Calories 373 | Fat 8g |Sodium 146mg | Carbs 8g | Fiber 5g | Sugar 1g | Protein 23g

EGG, AVOCADO, AND BACON SANDWICH

PREPARATION TIME: 15 MINUTES **COOKING TIME: 5 MINUTES** **SERVINGS: 1**

INGREDIENTS

- 1 croissant, sliced
- 2 bacon slices, cooked
- 1 slice Swiss cheese
- ¼ avocado, pitted and sliced
- 1 large egg
- 1 tablespoon basil pesto

PREPARATION:

1. Preheat your Hamilton Beach Breakfast Sandwich Maker.

2. Divide the pesto between the two halves of the croissant, spreading it evenly.

3. Place half of the croissant, pesto-side up, inside the bottom tray of the sandwich maker.

4. Arrange the slices of bacon on top of the bagel and top with the slice of Swiss cheese.

5. Slide the egg tray into place and crack the egg into it.

6. Top the egg with the other top half of the croissant, pesto-side down.

7. Cover the top hood, and let the sandwich cook for 5 minutes.

8. When finished cooking, rotate the handle of the cooking plate clockwise until it stops.

9. Lift the hood, the rings and transfer the sandwich to a plate.

NUTRITION FACTS:

Calories 288 | Fat 6.9g |Sodium 761mg | Carbs 46g | Fiber 4g | Sugar 12g | Protein 9.6g

EGG AND HAM SANDWICH

PREPARATION TIME: 15 MINUTES **COOKING TIME: 5 MINUTES** **SERVINGS: 1**

INGREDIENTS

- 2 slices whole grain bread, cut in 4-inch circle
- 2 slices deli ham
- 1 slice Swiss cheese
- 1 large egg
- 2 teaspoons heavy cream
- 1 teaspoon chopped chives

PREPARATION:

1. Preheat your Hamilton Beach Breakfast Sandwich Maker.

2. Place one slice of bread in the bottom tray of the sandwich maker.

3. Arrange the slices of ham on top of the bread and top with the slice of Swiss cheese.

4. Beat together the egg, heavy cream and chives in a small bowl.

5. Slide the egg tray into place over the cheese and pour the beaten egg mixture into the tray.

6. Top the egg mixture with the remaining slice of bread.

7. Cover the top hood, and let the sandwich cook for 5 minutes.

8. When finished cooking, rotate the handle of the cooking plate clockwise until it stops.

9. Lift the hood, the rings and transfer the sandwich to a plate.

★ Serving Suggestion: Serve the sandwich with coleslaw and your favorite sauce on the side.

★ Variation Tip: You can add a layer of your favorite sauce to the filling as well.

 **NUTRITION FACTS:**

Calories 350 | Fat 2.6g |Sodium 358mg | Carbs 64.6g | Fiber 14.4g | Sugar 3.3g | Protein 19.9g

STEAK & EGGS SANDWICH

PREPARATION TIME: 5 MINUTES | COOKING TIME: 5 MINUTES | SERVINGS: 1

INGREDIENTS

- 1 English muffin, split
- 1 – 2 tsp. creamy horseradish
- Thin strips of precooked steak
- A few fresh onion rings
- 1 slice smoked Gouda cheese
- 1 egg
- Sea salt and pepper

PREPARATION:

1. Spread the horseradish on both English muffin halves. Place one half into the bottom ring of breakfast sandwich maker, cut side up. Place

steak, onion and Gouda cheese on top.

2. Lower the cooking plate and top ring; crack an egg into the egg plate and pierce to break the yolk. Season with sea salt and pepper. Top with other muffin half.

3. Close the cover and cook for 4 to 5 minutes or until egg is cooked and cheese is melted. Remove sandwich with a rubber spatula and enjoy!

★ Serving Suggestion: Serve with a side of hash browns.

★ Variation Tip: Use a different type of cheese for a unique flavor.

 **NUTRITION FACTS:**

Calories 400 | Fat 20g |Sodium 500mg | Carbs 25g | Fiber 2g | Sugar 5g | Protein 25g

ALMOND PANCAKE WITH EGG AND PROSCIUTTO

PREPARATION TIME: 2 MINUTES | COOKING TIME: 4 MINUTES | SERVINGS: 1

INGREDIENTS

- 2 4-inch Almond Flour Pancakes, fresh or frozen
- 1 Egg
- 1 ounce chopped Prosciutto
- 1 ounce shredded Cheddar
- Salt and Pepper, to taste

PREPARATION:

1. Preheat the sandwich maker and grease it with some cooking spray.

2. Add one pancake to the bottom ring and top it with prosciutto and cheddar.

3. Lower the top ring and cooking plate, and crack the egg into it. Season with salt and pepper.

4. Add the second pancake on top and close the unit.

5. Cook for 3 minutes or 4 if using frozen pancakes.

6. Open carefully and transfer to a plate.

7. Serve and enjoy!

★ Serving Suggestion: Serve with a side of fresh fruit.

★ Variation Tip: Try using different types of cheeses or meats.

 **NUTRITION FACTS:**

Calories 430 | Total Fats 34.5g | Carbs 5.8g | Protein 25g | Fiber 1.3g

PESTO CHEESE SANDWICH

PREPARATION TIME: 5 MINUTES | COOKING TIME: 10 MINUTES | SERVINGS: 2

INGREDIENTS

- 4 Italian or French bread slices
- 3 tbsp. Pesto
- 2 red peppers, roasted
- 6 basil leaves, fresh
- 4 mozzarella slices, fresh
- 1 tbsp. Tomatoes, sun-dried
- 3 tbsp. Butter softened

PREPARATION:

1. Preheat the sandwich maker/Panini on medium-low.

2. Make the sandwich by layering the ingredients on one slice of bread and place the second on top.

3. Spread butter on both outer layers and cook on the Panini for 3 minutes.

4. Let it rest for 1 minute.

Cut and serve

★ Serving Suggestion: Serve with a side of pickles.

★ Variation Tip: Use different types of peppers for a change of flavor.

 **NUTRITION FACTS:**

Calories 400 | Fat 25g | Sodium 600mg | Carbs 30g | Fiber 2g | Sugar 5g | Protein 15g

PANCAKE, SAUSAGE & EGG SANDWICH

PREPARATION TIME: 2 MINUTES | COOKING TIME: 3 MINUTES | SERVINGS: 1

INGREDIENTS

- 2 small store bought or homemade pancakes
- Butter
- 1 sausage patty
- 1 slice cheddar cheese
- 1 egg

PREPARATION:

1. Butter each pancake and place one, butter side up, into the bottom ring of breakfast sandwich maker. Place sausage patty and cheddar cheese on top.

2. Lower the cooking plate and top ring; crack an egg into the egg plate and pierce to break the yolk; top with other buttered pancake.

3. Close the cover and cook for 4 to 5 minutes o

r until egg is cooked through. Gently slide the egg plate out and remove sandwich with a rubber spatula.

NUTRITION FACTS:

Calories 350 | Fat 20g | Sodium 550mg | Carbs 25g | Fiber 1g | Sugar 5g | Protein 18g

SAUSAGE MUFFIN SANDWICH

 **PREPARATION TIME: 15 MINUTES**   **COOKING TIME: 5 MINUTES**   **SERVINGS: 1**

INGREDIENTS

- 1 tablespoon unsalted butter
- 1 English muffin, split
- 1 breakfast sausage patty, cooked
- 2 slices American cheese
- 2 large eggs, beaten
- Salt and black pepper, to taste
- 1 handful of fresh chives, chopped
- Hot sauce and honey, for serving

PREPARATION:

. Beat eggs with black pepper, chives, salt, oney and hot sauce in a bowl.

2. Preheat your Hamilton Beach Breakfast andwich Maker until PREHEAT light gets green.

3. Lift the top cover, ring, and cooking plate.

4. Place half of the English muffin, cut-side up, nside the bottom tray of the sandwich maker. rush it with butter.

5. Add sausage patty on top.

---

6. Now lower the cooking plate and top rings, then pour in the egg.

7. Place a cheese slice and the other top half of the muffin on top.

8. Cover the top hood, and let the sandwich cook for 5 minutes.

9. Rotate the handle of the cooking plate clockwise until it stops.

10. Lift the hood, the rings and transfer the sandwich to a plate.

NUTRITION FACTS:

Calories 375 | Fat 16g |Sodium 255mg | Carbs 4.1g | Fiber 1.2g | Sugar 5g | Protein 24.1g

CREAMY SCRAMBLED EGG SANDWICH

 **PREPARATION TIME: 15 MINUTES**   **COOKING TIME: 5 MINUTES**   **SERVINGS: 2**

INGREDIENTS

- Scrambled eggs
- 4 large eggs
- 1 small pinch of cayenne pepper
- Kosher salt, to taste
- 2 tablespoons unsalted butter
- 3 tablespoons cream cheese
- Assembly
- 4 American cheese slices
- 4 thick potato bread slices, cut into 4 inches round

PREPARATION:

1. Beat egg with butter, cream cheese, cayenne pepper and salt in a bowl.

2. Preheat your Hamilton Beach Breakfast Sandwich Maker until PREHEAT light gets green.

3. Lift the top cover, ring, and cooking plate.

4. Place one bread slice, inside the bottom tray of the sandwich maker.

5. Now lower the cooking plate and top rings, then pour in ¼ the egg.

6. Place one cheese slice and the other bread slice on top.

7. Cover the top hood, and let the sandwich cook for 5 minutes.

8. Rotate the handle of the cooking plate clockwise until it stops.

9. Lift the hood, the rings and transfer the sandwich to a plate.

10. Repeat the same steps with the remaining ingredients.

★ Serving Suggestion: Serve the sandwich with a broccoli salad on the side.

★ Variation Tip: Add a layer of spicy mayo and pickled veggies for a change of taste.

 **NUTRITION FACTS:**

Calories 348 | Fat 12g |Sodium 710mg | Carbs 4g | Fiber 5g |Sugar 3g | Protein 31g

EGG-AND-CHEESE MUFFINS

PREPARATION TIME: 15 MINUTES

COOKING TIME: 5 MINUTES

SERVINGS: 2

INGREDIENTS

- 1 red onion, peeled, separated into rings
- 1 teaspoon soy sauce
- ½ teaspoons garlic powder
- 2 tablespoons olive oil
- Salt, to taste
- ¼ cup soft herbs, chopped
- 2 tablespoons green hot sauce
- 1 tablespoon unsalted butter
- 4 large eggs, beaten
- 2 whole-grain English muffins, toasted
- 2 ounces sharp cheddar cheese, sliced

PREPARATION:

1. Toss onion with soy sauce, garlic powder, olive oil, salt, herbs, and sauce in a bowl.

2. Preheat your Hamilton Beach Breakfast Sandwich Maker until PREHEAT light gets green.

3. Lift the top cover, ring, and cooking plate.

4. Place half of the English muffin, cut-side up, inside the bottom tray of the sandwich maker.

5. Brush its top with butter and add ½ of the onion mixture.

6. Now lower the cooking plate and top rings, then pour in ½ of the egg.

7. Place the cheese and other top half of the muffin on top and brush it with butter.

8. Cover the top hood, and let the muffin cook for 5 minutes.

9. Rotate the handle of the cooking plate clockwise until it stops.

10. Lift the hood, the rings and transfer the muffin to a plate.

11. Repeat the same steps with the remaining ingredients as well.

★ Serving Suggestion: Serve the sandwich with crispy fries on the side.

★ Variation Tip: Add a layer of pickled veggies for a change of taste.

 **NUTRITION FACTS:**

Calories 404 | Fat 13g |Sodium 216mg | Carbs 7g | Fiber 3g | Sugar 4g | Protein 31g

EGG, SPINACH, AND PARMESAN SANDWICH

PREPARATION TIME: 15 MINUTES | COOKING TIME: 5 MINUTES | SERVINGS: 1

INGREDIENTS

- 1 toasted English muffin, sliced
- ½ cup baby spinach leaves
- 2 large egg whites
- 1 tablespoon grated parmesan cheese
- 1 garlic clove, minced

PREPARATION:

1. Preheat your Hamilton Beach Breakfast Sandwich Maker.

2. Lift the top cover, ring, and cooking plate.

3. Place half of the English muffin, cut-side up, inside the bottom tray of the sandwich maker.

4. Arrange the baby spinach leaves on top of the English muffin.

5. Beat the egg whites, parmesan cheese and garlic in a small bowl.

6. Now lower the cooking plate and top rings then pour in the egg mixture.

7. Place the other top half of the muffin on top.

8. Cover the top hood, and let the sandwich cook for 5 minutes.

9. When finished cooking, rotate the handle of the cooking plate clockwise until it stops.

10. Lift the hood, the rings and transfer the sandwich to a plate.

★ Serving Suggestion: Serve the sandwich with crispy bacon and your favorite sauce on the side.

★ Variation Tip: You can add a lettuce leave to the filling as well.

NUTRITION FACTS:

Calories 282 | Fat 15g |Sodium 526mg | Carbs 20g | Fiber 0.6g | Sugar 3.3g | Protein 16g

HAM AND CHEDDAR MUFFIN

PREPARATION TIME: 15 MINUTES | COOKING TIME: 5 MINUTES | SERVINGS: 1

INGREDIENTS

- 1 toasted English muffin, sliced
- 2 slices deli ham
- 1 slice cheddar cheese
- 1 large egg, beaten

PREPARATION:

1. Preheat your Hamilton Beach Breakfast Sandwich Maker.

2. Lift the top cover, ring, and cooking plate.

3. Place the lower half of the muffin in the sandwich maker and top it with ham slices.

4. Now lower the cooking plate and top rings, then pour in the egg.

5. Place the cheese slice and top half of the bun on top.

6. Cover the top hood, and let the sandwich cook for 5 minutes.

7. When finished cooking, rotate the handle of the cooking plate clockwise until it stops.

8. Lift the hood, the rings and transfer the sandwich to a plate.

★ Serving Suggestion: Serve the sandwich with crispy bacon and your favorite sauce on the side.

★ Variation Tip: Add some additional ground black pepper to the filling.

 **NUTRITION FACTS:**

Calories 307 | Fat 8.6g |Sodium 510mg | Carbs 22.2g |
Fiber 1.4g | Sugar 13g | Protein 33.6g

EGGS-IN-A-HOLE SANDWICH WITH BACON

 **PREPARATION TIME: 15 MINUTES**   **COOKING TIME: 15 MINUTES**   **SERVINGS: 2**

INGREDIENTS

- 4 slices thick-cut bacon
- 4 ¾-inch-thick sourdough bread slices, cut into 4-inch round
- 4 large eggs
- Salt and black pepper, to taste
- 2 tablespoons unsalted butter
- 4 slices cheddar
- 4 teaspoons Hot sauce, for serving

PREPARATION:

1. Sauté bacon in a skillet for 5 minutes per side until golden brown.

2. Preheat your Hamilton Beach Breakfast Sandwich Maker until PREHEAT light gets green.

3. Lift the top cover, ring, and cooking plate.

4. Place a bread slice, inside the bottom tray of the sandwich maker.

5. Spread the butter on top of the bread.

6. Arrange 2 bacon slices on top of the English muffin.

7. Beat the egg with black pepper and salt in a small bowl.

8. Now lower the cooking plate and top rings, then pour in the egg.

9. Place a cheddar cheese slice and the other bread slice on top.

10. Cover the top hood, and let the sandwich cook for 5 minutes.

11. Rotate the handle of the cooking plate clockwise until it stops.

12. Lift the hood, the rings and transfer the sandwich to a plate.

13. Repeat the same step with the remaining ingredients.

★ Serving Suggestion: Serve the sandwich with a cauliflower bacon salad on the side.

★ Variation Tip: Enjoy sautéed veggies on the side for a change of taste.

 **NUTRITION FACTS:**

Calories 311 | Fat 12.5g |Sodium 595mg | Carbs 3g | Fiber 12g | Sugar 12g | Protein 17g

HAM AND CHEESE SANDWICH

 **PREPARATION TIME: 10 MINUTES** **COOKING TIME: 5 MINUTES** **SERVINGS: 1**

INGREDIENTS

- 2 slices of ham
- 1 cheese slice
- 1 egg
- 2 slices of bread
- 1 lettuce leaf

PREPARATION:

1. Preheat the breakfast machine first.

2. Break the eggs into the bottom baking tray, cover and fry until done.

3. Put in a slice of bread and spread with lettuce leaves, ham slices and cheese slices.

4. Put the fried egg on top and cover with another slice of bread.

5. Fasten the breakfast machine and wait a few minutes until the sandwiches are golden brown.

★ Serving Suggestion: Serve with a glass of hot milk.

★ Variation Tip: Tomato slices can be added to add texture.

NUTRITION FACTS:

Calories 300 | Fat 12g |Sodium 500mg | Carbs 25g | Fiber 1.5g | Sugar 5g | Protein. Nutritional information per serving: calories 300 | fat 12g | sodium 500mg | carbs 25g | fiber 1.5g | sugar 5g | protein 15g

GRILLED CHICKEN AND AVOCADO SANDWICH

PREPARATION TIME: 15 MINUTES | **COOKING TIME: 5 MINUTES** | **SERVINGS: 2**

INGREDIENTS

- 1 cup of shredded lettuce
- 1 ripe avocado
- 1 sliced tomato
- Black pepper and salt
- ¼ cup of jalapeno pepper, sliced
- 8 ounces of grilled chicken breast
- ⅔ cup of black beans, mashed
- 2 sandwich buns, split

PREPARATION:

1. Preheat your Hamilton Beach Breakfast Sandwich Maker.

2. Lift the top cover, ring, and cooking plate.

3. Place the lower half of a bun in the sandwich maker.

4. Now lower the cooking plate and top rings, then add ½ of the fillings.

5. Place the other top half of the bun on top.

6. Cover the top hood, and let the sandwich cook for 5 minutes.

7. When finished cooking, rotate the handle of the cooking plate clockwise until it stops.

8. Lift the hood, the rings and transfer the sandwich to a plate.

9. Repeat the same steps with remaining ingredients.

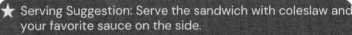

★ Serving Suggestion: Serve the sandwich with coleslaw and your favorite sauce on the side.

★ Variation Tip: Add some additional ground black pepper to the filling.

NUTRITION FACTS:

Calories 521 | Fat 17.1 g | Sodium 840mg | Carbs 65.5 g | Fiber 2.9 g | Sugar 2.6 g | Protein 26.1g

CHICKEN PESTO SANDWICH

PREPARATION TIME: 15 MINUTES | **COOKING TIME: 30 MINUTES** | **SERVINGS: 2**

INGREDIENTS

- 4 tbsp. Olive oil
- 2 chicken breasts, skinless and boneless
- 1 tsp. Oregano, dried
- ¼ tsp. Pepper fakes
- Black pepper and salt to taste
- 2 rolls, ciabatta
- ¼ cup of Pesto
- 1 sliced Tomato
- 4 oz. Mozzarella, fresh, sliced

PREPARATION:

1. Turn on medium heat and place a skillet. Add 2 tbsp. olive oil. While the oil heats season with chicken with black pepper, salt, pepper flakes, and oregano. Cook the chicken 7 minutes on each side. Set aside.

2. Now slice the rolls and spread pesto. Top with mozzarella, chicken, and tomato. Spread pesto again. Top with the other half of the roll.

PREPARATION:

3. Heat the sandwich press and coat with 2 tbsp. oil. Add one sandwich and press. Cook 5 minutes. Repeat with the second roll.

4. Serve and enjoy!

★ Serving Suggestion: Serve with a side of potato chips.

★ Variation Tip: Add some sliced avocado for extra creaminess.

NUTRITION FACTS:

Calories 550 | Fat 30g | Sodium 800mg | Carbs 35g | Fiber 3g | Sugar 5g | Protein 30g

CHICKEN AND BACON PAPRIKA SANDWICH

PREPARATION TIME: 5 MINUTES | COOKING TIME: 4 MINUTES | SERVINGS: 1

INGREDIENTS

- 1 ounce ground Chicken
- 1 ounce cooked and crumbled Bacon
- ¼ tsp smoked Paprika
- 2 Red Pepper Rings
- 1 slice of Cheese
- 1 tsp chopped Onion
- 2 tsp Dijon Mustard
- 1 small Hamburger Bun

PREPARATION:

1. Preheat the sandwich maker until the green light appears and grease it with some cooking spray.

2. Cut the hamburger bun in half and brush the insides with the mustard.

3. Place one half with the mustard-side up, on top of the bottom ring.

---

4. Add the chicken and bacon and sprinkle the paprika over.

5. Top with the pepper, onion, and add the cheese on top.

6. Lower the top ring and finish it off by adding the second bun, placed with the mustard-side down.

7. Close the lid and cook for 4 minutes.

8. Open the lid with mittens, and carefully transfer to a plate.

9. Serve and enjoy!

★ Serving Suggestion: Serve with a small pickle spear.

★ Variation Tip: Use a different type of cheese for variety.

NUTRITION FACTS:

Calories 298 | Total Fats 13g | Carbs 21g | Protein 23.5g | Fiber 5.5g

SPINACH AND PESTO CHICKEN PANINI

PREPARATION TIME: 10 MINUTES | COOKING TIME: 5 MINUTES | SERVINGS: 1

INGREDIENTS

- 1/2 cup mayonnaise
- 2 tablespoons prepared pesto
- 1 1/2 cups shredded rotisserie chicken
- Kosher salt
- Freshly ground pepper
- 1 1lb. Ciabatta loaf, split lengthwise and cut into 4 pieces
- Extra-virgin olive oil, for brushing
- 1 cup lightly packed baby spinach
- 8 thin slices of Swiss cheese

PREPARATION:

1. Use a whisk to combine the pesto and mayonnaise. Then mix in the chicken and salt and pepper to taste.

2. Use a brush to coat the top and bottom of the bread with olive oil. Put a layer of chicken on the bottom piece of bread, then spinach, and finally cheese. Place the top piece of bread on the cheese.

3. Cook the sandwiches for 7 minutes on medium heat, and make sure to flip halfway through. The bread should be brown, and the cheese should be melted.

★ Serving Suggestion: Serve with a side of fruit salad.

★ Variation Tip: Add some sliced mushrooms for an earthy flavor.

NUTRITION FACTS:

Calories 600 | Fat 35g | Sodium 900mg | Carbs 40g | Fiber 4g | Sugar 6g | Protein 35g

CHEESY CHICKEN WAFFLE SANDWICH

PREPARATION TIME: 5 MINUTES | COOKING TIME: 4 MINUTES | SERVINGS: 1

INGREDIENTS

- A couple of thin cooked Chicken Slices, about 2 – 3 ounces in total
- 1 slice American or Cheddar Cheese
- 1 Prosciutto Slice
- 2 tomato Slices
- 2 tsp Mayonnaise
- 2 Frozen Waffles

PREPARATION:

1. Preheat and grease the sandwich maker.

2. Cut the waffles into 4 - inch circles so that they can fit inside the unit.

3. Place one waffle on top of the bottom ring.

4. Add the chicken, place the tomato slices on top, and spread the mayo over.

5. Top with the prosciutto and finish it off by adding the slice of cheese.

6. Lower the top ring and add the second waffle.

7. Close the unit and cook for 4 ½ minutes.

8. Serve and enjoy!

★ Serving Suggestion: Serve with a side of maple syrup.

★ Variation Tip: Use different types of cheese for a unique flavor.

NUTRITION FACTS:

Calories 350 | Total Fats 28g | Carbs 22g | Protein 24g | Fiber 2g

LEMONY CHICKEN AND CHEERY SANDWICH

PREPARATION TIME: 15 MINUTES | COOKING TIME: 5 MINUTES | SERVINGS: 1

INGREDIENTS

- 1 teaspoon of lemon juice
- 1 green onion
- Lettuce leaves
- 2 teaspoons of mayonnaise
- 2 tablespoons of dried tart cherries
- 1 croissant split
- Black pepper
- 1 cup of cooked chicken
- ⅛ cup of plain yogurt
- 1 teaspoon of chopped parsley

PREPARATION:

1. Mix lemon juice, mayonnaise, pepper, and yogurt in a bowl
2. Preheat your Hamilton Beach Breakfast Sandwich Maker.
3. Lift the top cover, ring, and cooking plate.
4. Place the lower half of a croissant in the sandwich maker.
5. Now lower the cooking plate and top rings, then add the remaining fillings.
6. Place the other top half of the croissant on top.
7. Cover the top hood, and let the sandwich cook for 5 minutes.
8. When finished cooking, rotate the handle of the cooking plate clockwise until it stops.
9. Lift the hood, the rings and transfer the sandwich to a plate.

★ Serving Suggestion: Serve the sandwich with your favorite sauce on the side.

★ Variation Tip: You can add a lettuce leave to the filling as well.

 **NUTRITION FACTS:**

Calories 524 | Fat 24 g | Sodium 568 mg | Carbs 24 g | Fiber 9 g | Sugar 5.2g | Protein 24

THE ULTIMATE CHICKEN, SPINACH AND MOZZARELLA SANDWICH

PREPARATION TIME: 5 MINUTES | COOKING TIME: 4 MINUTES | SERVINGS: 1

INGREDIENTS

- 1 small Hamburger Bun
- 3 ounces cooked and chopped Chicken
- 1 tbsp Cream Cheese
- 1 ounce shredded Mozzarella
- 1 tbsp canned Corn
- 2 tbsp chopped Spinach

PREPARATION:

1. Preheat and grease the sandwich maker.
2. Cut the bun in half and brush the cream cheese on the insides.
3. Add one half to the bottom ring, with the cut-side up.
4. Place the chicken on top and top with the spinach, corn, and mozzarella.
5. Lower the top ring and add the second half of the bun, the cut-side down.
6. Cook for 4 minutes.
7. Rotate clockwise and lift to open.
8. Serve and enjoy!

★ Serving Suggestion: Serve with a side of potato chips.

★ Variation Tip: Add some sliced tomatoes for extra freshness.

 **NUTRITION FACTS:**

Calories 402 | Total Fats 15.5g | Carbs 32g | Protein 32.5g | Fiber 1.4g

BACON CHIPOTLE CHICKEN PANINI

 PREPARATION TIME: 5 MINUTES | COOKING TIME: 5 MINUTES | SERVINGS: 1

INGREDIENTS

- 2 slices sourdough bread
- 1/4 cup Caesar salad dressing
- 1 cooked chicken breast, diced
- 1/2 cup shredded Cheddar cheese
- 1 tablespoon bacon bits
- 1 1/2 teaspoons chipotle chili powder, or to taste
- 2 tablespoons softened butter

PREPARATION:

1. Spread the salad dressing on one side of both pieces of bread. Then top the dressing side of one piece of bread with chicken, then cheese, then bacon, and finally chipotle chili powder. Place the other piece of bread with the dressing side down on top. Butter the other side of both pieces of bread.

2. Cook the Panini on medium heat for 5 minutes, flipping halfway through. The bread should be brown, and the cheese should be melted.

★ Serving Suggestion: Serve with a side of pickles.

★ Variation Tip: Use a different type of cheese for a unique flavor.

NUTRITION FACTS:

Calories 650 | Fat 40g | Sodium 1200mg | Carbs 40g | Fiber 2g | Sugar 5g | Protein 30g

BRUSCHETTA TURKEY PANINI

PREPARATION TIME: 15 MINUTES | COOKING TIME: 4 MINUTES | SERVINGS: 4

INGREDIENTS

- 8 slices Italian bread
- 8 fresh basil leaves
- 8 thinly sliced tomatoes
- 16 slices of Black Pepper Turkey Breast
- 4 pieces of mozzarella cheese
- 4 tablespoons mayonnaise
- Olive oil

PREPARATION:

1. Cut the basil into ribbons.

2. Place a layer of turkey on a piece of bread, then basil, and then cheese. Spread the mayo on the bottom part of the top piece of bread, and place it on top of the cheese. Brush the top and bottom of the sandwich with olive oil

3. Cook the sandwiches for 4 minutes on medium heat, and make sure to flip halfway through. The bread should be brown, and the cheese should be melted.

★ Serving Suggestion: Serve with a side of pasta salad.

★ Variation Tip: Add some roasted red peppers for extra flavor.

NUTRITION FACTS:

Calories 450 | Fat 20g | Sodium 750mg | Carbs 40g | Fiber 3g | Sugar 5g | Protein 25g

CHICKEN BURGER

PREPARATION TIME: 25 MINUTES | COOKING TIME: 15 MINUTES | SERVINGS: 1

INGREDIENTS

- 1 chicken breast
- Two hamburger buns
- Proper onion rings
- Pickle slices to taste
- Moderate tomato sauce
- Mayonnaise in moderation
- Salt and pepper to taste

PREPARATION:

1. Cut the chicken breasts into small pieces and marinate with salt and black pepper for 20 minutes.
2. Fry the marinated chicken breasts in a sandwich machine and mash.
3. Spread ketchup and mayonnaise on the bottom of the burger bun.
4. Add lettuce, onion rings, pickles and fried chicken pieces.
5. Cover the top of the burger bun and heat slightly in a sandwich maker for a firmer burger.

★ Serving Suggestion: Serve with French fries.

★ Variation Tip: Add a slice of cheese for extra richness.

NUTRITION FACTS:

Calories 450 | Fat 15g | Sodium 600mg | Carbs 50g | Fiber 3g | Sugar 8g | Protein 25g

MUSHROOM, TURKEY, AND SWISS CHEESE BURGERS

 PREPARATION TIME: 15 MINUTES COOKING TIME: 15 MINUTES SERVINGS: 4

INGREDIENTS

- 2 tablespoons olive oil
- 1 garlic clove, minced
- ¾ teaspoon black pepper
- ½ teaspoon salt
- 8 Portobello mushroom caps
- 1 lb. lean ground turkey
- 2 teaspoons Worcestershire sauce
- 1 teaspoon Dijon mustard
- 4 slices Swiss cheese
- 1 small tomato, sliced
- 3 cups baby arugula

PREPARATION:

1. Blend turkey with garlic, black pepper, salt, and Worcestershire sauce in a food processor for 1 minute.
2. Set a suitable skillet with olive oil over medium-high heat.
3. Make 4 equal-sized patties out of the turkey mixture.
4. Sear the turkey patties in the oil for 5 minutes per side.
5. Preheat your Hamilton Beach Breakfast Sandwich Maker until PREHEAT light gets green.
6. Lift the top cover, ring, and cooking plate.
7. Place a Portobello mushroom cap, cut-side up, inside the bottom tray of the sandwich maker.
8. Now lower the cooking plate and top rings then place a patty, ¼ Swiss cheese, tomato, and arugula on top.
9. Place the other mushroom cap on top.
10. Cover the top hood, and let the sandwich cook for 5 minutes.
11. Rotate the handle of the cooking plate clockwise until it stops.
12. Lift the hood, the rings and transfer the sandwich to a plate.
13. Repeat the same steps with the remaining ingredients.

★ Serving Suggestion: Serve the sandwich with crispy sweet potato fries on the side.

★ Variation Tip: You could add some sautéed onions for extra flavor.

NUTRITION FACTS:

Calories 380 | Fat 18g | Sodium 650mg | Carbs 12g | Fiber 4g | Sugar 5g | Protein 35g

HERBED CHICKEN AND ONION BURGER

PREPARATION TIME: 15 MINUTES | COOKING TIME: 15 MINUTES | SERVINGS: 8

INGREDIENTS

- 2 tablespoons olive oil
- ½ medium red onion, minced
- 4 garlic cloves, minced
- 2 lbs. ground chicken meat
- ½ teaspoon salt
- 1 teaspoon black pepper
- ½ cup chopped parsley
- 1 tablespoon fresh rosemary
- 1 tablespoon fresh sage
- 2 teaspoons fresh thyme, chopped
- 8 burger buns, split in half
- 1 onion, sliced
- 8 lettuce leaves
- 8 tomato slices
- 8 bacon slices, cooked

PREPARATION:

1. Blend chicken with red onion, garlic, salt, black pepper, parsley, rosemary, sage and thyme in a food processor for 1 minute.

2. Set a suitable skillet with olive oil over medium-high heat.

3. Make eight equal-sized patties out of the turkey mixture.

4. Sear the chicken patties in the oil for 5 minutes per side

5. Preheat your Hamilton Beach Breakfast Sandwich Maker until PREHEAT light gets green.

6. Lift the top cover, ring, and cooking plate.

7. Place half of a bun, cut-side up, inside the bottom tray of the sandwich maker.

8. Now lower the cooking plate and top rings, then place a patty, an onion slice, a lettuce leaf and a tomato slice on top.

9. Place the other top half of the bun on top.

10. Cover the top hood, and let the sandwich cook for 5 minutes.

★ Serving Suggestion: Serve with a side of coleslaw.

★ Variation Tip: Add some cheese slices for a gooey texture.

NUTRITION FACTS:

Calories 420 | Fat 18g | Sodium 680mg | Carbs 35g | Fiber 2g | Sugar 6g | Protein 28g

TURKEY BURGERS WITH HONEY AND MUSTARD

PREPARATION TIME: 15 MINUTES | COOKING TIME: 15 MINUTES | SERVINGS: 4

INGREDIENTS

- ¼ cup mustard
- 2 tablespoons honey
- 1 lb. ground turkey breast
- ¼ teaspoon salt
- ¼ teaspoon black pepper
- 2 teaspoons canola oil
- 4 whole-wheat hamburger buns, split
- 4 lettuce leaves
- 4 tomato slices
- 4 red onion slices

PREPARATION:

1. Blend turkey with salt, honey, mustard and black pepper in a food processor for 1 minute.

2. Set a suitable skillet with olive oil over

medium-high heat.

3. Make 4 equal-sized patties out of the turkey mixture.

4. Sear the turkey patties in the oil for 5 minutes per side.

5. Preheat your Hamilton Beach Breakfast Sandwich Maker until PREHEAT light gets green.

6. Lift the top cover, ring, and cooking plate.

7. Place half of a bun, cut-side up, inside the bottom tray of the sandwich maker.

8. Now lower the cooking plate and top rings then place a patty, a lettuce leaf, 1 onion slice and tomato slice on top.

9. Place the other top half of the bun on top.

10. Cover the top hood, and let the sandwich cook for 5 minutes.

11. Rotate the handle of the cooking plate clockwise until it stops.

12. Lift the hood, the rings and transfer the sandwich to a plate.

13. Repeat the same steps with the remaining ingredients.

★ Serving Suggestion: Serve the sandwich with crispy bacon and your favorite sauce on the side.
★ Variation Tip: You could add some sliced avocado for a creamier texture.

 **NUTRITION FACTS:**

Calories 380 | Fat 12g | Sodium 550mg | Carbs 40g | Fiber 5g | Sugar 8g | Protein 25g

CHICKEN AND AVOCADO PITA SANDWICH

 PREPARATION TIME: 15 MINUTES
 COOKING TIME: 5 MINUTES
 SERVINGS: 1

INGREDIENTS

- 1 pita bread, split, cut in 4-inch circle
- 1 small onion
- 1 teaspoon of lemon juice
- ¼ teaspoons of salt
- 2 tablespoons of Monterey Jack cheese, shredded
- 1 teaspoon of vegetable oil
- 1 tablespoon of taco sauce
- ½ cup of cooked chicken
- ½ cup of shredded lettuce
- 1 ounce of green chilies
- 1 tablespoon of sour cream
- 1 small sliced avocado

PREPARATION:

1. Sprinkle salt and lemon juice on avocado

2. Mix onion, salt, chilies, oil, taco sauce, and chicken together

3. Top with the avocado mix, lettuce, and cheese

4. Preheat your Hamilton Beach Breakfast Sandwich Maker.

5. Lift the top cover, ring, and cooking plate.

6. Place one bread round in the sandwich maker.

7. Now lower the cooking plate and top rings, then add the fillings on top.

8. Add the other circle of the bread on top.

9. Cover the top hood, and let the sandwich cook for 5 minutes.

10. When finished cooking, rotate the handle of the cooking plate clockwise until it stops.

11. Lift the hood, the rings and transfer the sandwich to a plate.

★ Serving Suggestion: Serve the sandwich with your favorite sauce on the side.
★ Variation Tip: You can add a layer of your favorite sauce to the filling as well.

 **NUTRITION FACTS:**

Calories 480 | Fat 20g | Sodium 700mg | Carbs 50g | Fiber 6g | Sugar 8g | Protein 22g

MAYO CHICKEN SALAD SANDWICH

PREPARATION TIME: 15 MINUTES | COOKING TIME: 5 MINUTES | SERVINGS: 1

INGREDIENTS

- 1 teaspoon of lemon juice
- 2 multigrain bread, cut in 4-inch circle
- 1 tablespoon of mayonnaise
- 2 pound of chicken breast
- 1 teaspoon of fresh dill
- 2 lettuce leaves
- ⅛ teaspoons of salt
- 1 tablespoon of plain yogurt
- ⅛ teaspoons of grated lemon zest

PREPARATION:

1. Mix dill, lemon juice, mayonnaise, salt, yogurt, and lemon zest in a bowl.

2. Preheat your Hamilton Beach Breakfast Sandwich Maker.

3. Lift the top cover, ring, and cooking plate.

4. Place one bread round in the sandwich maker.

5. Now lower the cooking plate and top rings, then add the lettuce leaves, chicken and sauce on top.

6. Add the other circle of the bread on top.

7. Cover the top hood, and let the sandwich cook for 5 minutes.

8. When finished cooking, rotate the handle of the cooking plate clockwise until it stops.

9. Lift the hood, the rings and transfer the sandwich to a plate.

★ Serving Suggestion: Serve the sandwich with your favorite sauce on the side.
★ Variation Tip: Add some additional dried herbs to the filling.

 **NUTRITION FACTS:**

Calories 340 | Fat 15.5g | Sodium 404mg | Carbs 18.3g | Fiber 2g | Sugar 2.7g | Protein 30.9g

CHICKEN CORDON BLEU SANDWICH

PREPARATION TIME: 15 MINUTES | COOKING TIME: 5 MINUTES | SERVINGS: 1

INGREDIENTS

- 1 ounce of chicken patties, cooked
- 1 split buns
- 1 sliced tomato
- 1 slice of Swiss cheese
- Mustard
- 1 slice of ham
- lettuce

PREPARATION:

1. Preheat your Hamilton Beach Breakfast Sandwich Maker.

2. Lift the top cover, ring, and cooking plate.

3. Place the lower half of a bun in the sandwich maker.

4. Now lower the cooking plate and top rings, then add all the fillings.

5. Place the other top half of the bun on top.

6. Cover the top hood, and let the sandwich cook for 5 minutes.

7. When finished cooking, rotate the handle of the cooking plate clockwise until it stops.

8. Lift the hood, the rings and transfer the sandwich to a plate.

NUTRITION FACTS:

Calories 386 | Fat 17g | Sodium 525mg | Carbs 36.1g | Fiber 2.6g | Sugar 2.2g | Protein 21g

BASIL CHICKEN BURGER WITH PIZZA SAUCE

PREPARATION TIME: 15 MINUTES | COOKING TIME: 5 MINUTES | SERVINGS: 2

INGREDIENTS

- 2 buns, split
- ½ teaspoon of basil
- 4 ounces of ground chicken
- 2 slices of provolone cheese
- 1 cup of pizza sauce

PREPARATION:

1. Top with 1 slice of provolone cheese, dried basil, and pizza sauce

2. Preheat your Hamilton Beach Breakfast Sandwich Maker.

3. Lift the top cover, ring, and cooking plate.

4. Place the lower half of a bun in the sandwich maker.

5. Now lower the cooking plate and top rings, then add ½ of the fillings.

6. Place the other top half of the bun on top.

7. Cover the top hood, and let the sandwich cook for 5 minutes.

8. When finished cooking, rotate the handle of the cooking plate clockwise until it stops.

9. Lift the hood, the rings and transfer the sandwich to a plate.

10. Repeat the same steps with remaining ingredients.

NUTRITION FACTS:

Calories 327 | Fat 18.3g | Sodium 512mg | Carbs 4.2g | Fiber 0.5g | Sugar 0.3g | Protein 35.3g

MAYO TURKEY BURGER

PREPARATION TIME: 15 MINUTES | COOKING TIME: 5 MINUTES | SERVINGS: 1

INGREDIENTS

- 1 lb. ground turkey
- 1 large egg, beaten
- 2 garlic cloves, minced
- 1 tablespoon Worcestershire sauce
- 2 tablespoons parsley, chopped
- Kosher salt, to taste
- Black pepper, to taste
- 1 tablespoon olive oil
- 6 Hamburger buns, cut in half
- 6 Lettuce leaves
- 6 tomato slices
- 6 teaspoon Mayonnaise

PREPARATION:

1. Blend turkey with egg, garlic, Worcestershire sauce, parsley, black pepper, and salt in a food processor for 1 minute.

2. Set a suitable skillet with olive oil over medium-high heat.

3. Make six equal-sized patties out of the turkey

mixture.

4. Sear the turkey patties in the oil for 5 minutes per side.

5. Preheat your Hamilton Beach Breakfast Sandwich Maker until PREHEAT light gets green.

6. Lift the top cover, ring, and cooking plate.

7. Place half of a bun, cut-side up, inside the bottom tray of the sandwich maker.

8. Now lower the cooking plate and top rings then place a patty, a lettuce leaf, and a tomato slice on top.

9. Place the other top half of the bun on top.

10. Cover the top hood, and let the sandwich cook for 5 minutes.

11. Rotate the handle of the cooking plate clockwise until it stops.

12. Lift the hood, the rings and transfer the sandwich to a plate.

13. Repeat the same steps with the remaining ingredients.

★ Serving Suggestion: Serve the sandwich with crispy zucchini fries on the side.
★ Variation Tip: you can add a lettuce leaf to the filling as well.

 NUTRITION FACTS:

Calories 448 | Fat 13g | Sodium 353mg | Carbs 23g | Fiber 0.4g | Sugar 1g | Protein 29g

TURKEY BURGER WITH TZATZIKI SAUCE

PREPARATION TIME: 15 MINUTES   COOKING TIME: 15 MINUTES   SERVINGS: 6

INGREDIENTS

- 2 lbs. ground turkey
- 2 teaspoons oregano
- 4 garlic cloves, minced
- 1 small onion, grated
- ¼ cup parsley, chopped
- 1 teaspoon cumin
- 1 teaspoon black pepper
- 2 teaspoons salt
- 2 tablespoons olive oil
- Tzatziki sauce
- 1 cup Greek yoghurt
- ½ English cucumber, grated
- 1 tablespoon dried dill or 2 tablespoons fresh dill
- 2 teaspoons za'atar, optional
- 1-2 garlic cloves, minced
- ½ teaspoons salt
- ¼ teaspoons pepper

Burger
- 6 romaine lettuce leaves
- 2 tomatoes, sliced
- 4 ounces feta, crumbled
- 6 hamburger buns, toasted
- 1 cup tzatziki sauce

PREPARATION:

1. Mix all the tzatziki sauce ingredients in a bowl and keep it aside.

2. Blend turkey with oregano, garlic, onion, parsley, cumin, black pepper, and salt in a food processor for 1 minute.

3. Set a suitable skillet with olive oil over medium-high heat.

4. Make six equal-sized patties out of the turkey mixture.

5. Sear the turkey patties in the oil for 5 minutes per side.

6. Preheat your Hamilton Beach Breakfast Sandwich Maker until PREHEAT light gets green.

7. Lift the top cover, ring, and cooking plate.

8. Place half of a bun, cut-side up, inside the

bottom tray of the sandwich maker.

9. Now lower the cooking plate and top rings then place a patty, a lettuce leaf, a tomato slice, ⅙ feta and tzatziki sauce on top.

10. Place the other top half of the bun on top.

11. Cover the top hood, and let the sandwich cook for 5 minutes.

12. Rotate the handle of the cooking plate clockwise until it stops.

13. Lift the hood, the rings and transfer the sandwich to a plate.

14. Repeat the same steps with the remaining ingredients.

★ Serving Suggestion: Serve the sandwich with crispy fries on the side.
★ Variation Tip: Add a layer of sliced bell peppers for a change of taste.

 **NUTRITION FACTS:**

Calories 345 | Fat 36g | Sodium 272mg | Carbs 41g | Fiber 0.2g | Sugar 0.1g | Protein 22.5g

NUTRITION FACTS:

Calories 420 | Total Fats 25g | Carbs 28g | Protein 23g | Fiber 5g

BEEF AND VEGGIES BAGEL SANDWICH

PREPARATION TIME: 5 MINUTES | **COOKING TIME: 3 MINUTES** | **SERVINGS: 1**

INGREDIENTS

- 1 tsp canned Peas
- 1 tsp canned Corn
- 1 tsp chopped Celery
- 1 tsp chopped Onion
- 1 Tomato Slice, chopped
- 2 ounces cooked Beef Roast, chopped
- 1 tbsp Sandwich Sauce
- 1 tbsp Cream Cheese
- 1 Bagel

PREPARATION:

1. Preheat the sandwich maker and grease it with some cooking spray.

2. Cut the bagel in half and spread the cream cheese over.

3. Place one half of the bagel on top of the bottom ring, with the spread-side up.

4. Top with the beef and veggies, and drizzle the sauce over

5. Lower the top ring and add the second bagel half inside, with the cream cheese down.

6. Close the lid and cook for 3 minutes.

7. Rotate clockwise and open carefully.

8. Serve and enjoy!

MAYO ROASTED BEEF MUFFIN SANDWICHES

PREPARATION TIME: 15 MINUTES | **COOKING TIME: 5 MINUTES** | **SERVINGS: 6**

INGREDIENTS

- 1 red onion, sliced thinly
- 1 tablespoon, plus 2 teaspoons salt
- 6 tablespoons red wine vinegar
- ¾ cup mayonnaise
- ¾ cup sour cream
- ¼ cup plus 2 tablespoons jarred grated horseradish (with liquid)
- ½ teaspoon grated lemon zest
- Freshly ground black pepper
- Hot sauce
- 6 English muffins, cut in half
- 12 slices ripened tomatoes
- 24 ounces freshly sliced rare roast beef
- 3 cups watercress or arugula

PREPARATION:

1. In a small bowl, mix onion and 1 tablespoon salt. Set aside for 20 minutes.

2. Rinse the onions with cold running water. Drain and squeeze to remove excess liquid.

3. Combine the onions and the vinegar and marinate at least 30 minutes or up to 24 hours.

4. In a small bowl, mix together the mayonnaise, sour cream, hot sauce, black pepper, horseradish, zest, and 2 teaspoon salt.

5. Then refrigerate the horseradish sauce for 30 minutes at least.

6. Preheat your Hamilton Beach Breakfast Sandwich Maker.

7. Lift the top cover, ring, and cooking plate.

8. Place the lower half of a muffin in the sandwich maker.

9. Top it with ⅙ of the filling ingredients except beef.

10. Now lower the cooking plate and top rings then place the ⅙th of the beef on top.

11. Place the other top half of a muffin on top.

12. Cover the top hood, and let the sandwich cook for 5 minutes.

13. When finished cooking, rotate the handle of the cooking plate clockwise until it stops.

14. Lift the hood, the rings and transfer the sandwich to a plate.

15. Repeat the same with remaining ingredients.

★ Serving Suggestion: Serve the sandwich with crispy bacon and your favorite sauce on the side.

★ Variation Tip: You can add a lettuce leave to the filling as well.

 **NUTRITION FACTS:**

Calories 260 | Fat 16g | Sodium 585mg | Carbs 3.1g | Fiber 1.3g | Sugar 0.2g | Protein 25.5g

PESTO BEEF AND MOZZARELLA PANINI

PREPARATION TIME: 15 MINUTES | COOKING TIME: 5 MINUTES | SERVINGS: 4

INGREDIENTS

- 8 slices Italian bread, 1/2 inch thick
- 2 tablespoons butter or margarine, softened
- 1/2 cup basil pesto
- 1/2 lb. thinly sliced cooked deli roast beef
- 4 slices (1 oz. each) mozzarella cheese
- Marinara sauce, warmed, if desired

PREPARATION:

1. Spread the pesto on one side of each piece of bread. Spread the butter on the other side.

2. Split the roast beef between four pieces of bread with the pesto side up and then top with the mozzarella. Place the other piece of bread on the mozzarella with the butter side up.

3. Cook the Panini on medium heat for 5 minutes, flipping halfway through. The bread should be brown, and the cheese should be melted.

★ Serving Suggestion: Serve with a side of salad.

★ Variation Tip: Add some sliced tomatoes for extra flavor.

 **NUTRITION FACTS:**

Calories 450 | Fat 25g | Sodium 600mg | Carbs 35g | Fiber 2g | Sugar 5g | Protein 20g

AUTHENTIC PHILLY STEAK SANDWICH

PREPARATION TIME: 15 MINUTES | COOKING TIME: 15 MINUTES | SERVINGS: 2

INGREDIENTS

- 1 lb. beef sirloin, cut into thin 2 inch strips
- ½ teaspoon salt
- ½ teaspoon black pepper
- ½ teaspoon paprika
- ½ teaspoon chili powder
- ½ teaspoon onion powder
- ½ teaspoon garlic powder
- ½ teaspoon dried thyme
- ½ teaspoon dried marjoram
- ½ teaspoon dried basil
- 3 tablespoons vegetable oil
- 1 onion, sliced
- 1 green bell pepper, julienned
- 3 ounces Swiss cheese, sliced
- 4 hamburger buns, split lengthwise

PREPARATION:

1. Sauté beef with all the spices, herbs, oil, onion and bell pepper in a skillet for 10 minutes.
2. Preheat your Hamilton Beach Breakfast Sandwich Maker until PREHEAT light gets green.
3. Lift the top cover, ring, and cooking plate.
4. Place half of a bun, cut-side up, inside the bottom tray of the sandwich maker.
5. Now lower the cooking plate and top rings then add ¼ of the beef mixture.
6. Place the cheese and other top half of a bun on top.
7. Cover the top hood, and let the sandwich cook for 5 minutes.
8. Rotate the handle of the cooking plate clockwise until it stops.
9. Lift the hood, the rings and transfer the sandwich to a plate.
10. Repeat the same steps with the remaining ingredients.

★ Serving Suggestion: Serve the sandwich with crispy carrot chips on the side.
★ Variation Tip: You could add some mushrooms for an earthy flavor.

NUTRITION FACTS:

Calories 401 | Fat 7g |Sodium 269mg | Carbs 5g | Fiber 4g | Sugar 12g | Protein 26g

BOLOGNESE CUP

PREPARATION TIME: 5 MINUTES | COOKING TIME: 3 MINUTES | SERVINGS: 1

INGREDIENTS

- 1 Flour Tortilla
- 2 ounces ground Beef, cooked
- 1 tsp chopped Onion
- 1 tbsp Marinara Sauce
- 1 ounce shredded Mozzarella Cheese

PREPARATION:

1. Preheat the sandwich maker and grease it with some cooking spray.
2. Add the tortilla inside, tucking it in, until it looks like a cup.
3. Add the beef, onion, and marinara sauce inside. Stir a bit to combine.
4. Top with the shredded mozzarella cheese.
5. Close the sandwich maker and cook for 3 ½ minutes.
6. Open the lid and transfer to a plate.

★ Serve and enjoy!Serving Suggestion: Serve with a side of garlic bread.
★ Variation Tip: Add some sliced mushrooms for extra texture.

NUTRITION FACTS:

Calories 375 | Total Fats 24g | Carbs 20g | Protein 19g | Fiber 1.4g

BEEF, WAFFLE, AND EGG SANDWICH

THE ULTIMATE 4-MINUTE CHEESEBURGER

 PREPARATION TIME: 5 MINUTES
 COOKING TIME: 4 MINUTES
 SERVINGS: 1
 PREPARATION TIME: 5 MINUTES
 COOKING TIME: 4 MINUTES
 SERVINGS: 1

INGREDIENTS

- 1 frozen Beef Pattie
- 2 4-inch Waffles
- 1 Egg, whisked
- ¼ tsp Garlic Powder
- Salt and Pepper, to taste
- 1 slice Cheddar Cheese

PREPARATION:

1. Preheat the unit until the green light appears. Grease with cooking spray.

2. Add one waffle to the bottom ring.

3. Add the beef pattie on top and top with the cheddar.

4. Lower the cooking plate and add the egg to it. Season with salt, pepper, and garlic powder.

5. Close the unit and cook for 4 minutes, not less.

6. Rotate the handles clockwise, lift to open, and carefully transfer to a plate.

7. Serve and enjoy!

★ Serving Suggestion:Serve with a side of hash browns.

★ Variation Tip:Replace the cheddar cheese with Swiss cheese for a different flavor.

 **NUTRITION FACTS:**

Calories 562 | Total Fats 38g | Carbs 28g | Protein 38g | Fiber 3g

INGREDIENTS

- 1 frozen Beef Patty
- 1 small Hamburger Bun
- 1 slice American Cheese
- 1 ounce cooked and crumbled Bacon
- 1 tsp Pickle Relish
- 2 Tomato Slices
- 1 tsp Dijon Mustard

PREPARATION:

1. Preheat the sandwich maker and grease it with some cooking spray.

2. Cut the bun in half and place one on top of the bottom ring.

3. Add the patty on top and brush with the mustard.

4. Top with bacon, pickle relish, and tomato slices.

5. Place the cheese on top.

6. Lower the top ring and add the second bun half.

7. Close the unit and cook for 4 minutes.

8. Open carefully and transfer to a plate.

9. Serve and enjoy!

★ Serving Suggestion:Serve with a side of crispy fries.

★ Variation Tip:Add some sliced onions for an extra flavor boost.

SPICY BEEF MUFFIN DELIGHT

PREPARATION TIME: 5 MINUTES | COOKING TIME: 4 MINUTES | SERVINGS: 1

INGREDIENTS

- 2 ounces cooked ground Beef
- 1 English Muffin
- ¼ tsp Chili Powder
- 1 tbsp chopped Tomatoes
- 2 tsp Beans

PREPARATION:

1. Grease your Hamilton Beach Breakfast Sandwich Maker and preheat it.
2. Cut the muffin in half.
3. When the green light appears, add one muffin half with the cut-side down, to the bottom ring.
4. In a small bowl, combine the tomatoes, beans, chili powder, and beef.
5. Top the muffin half with the beef mixture.
6. Lower the top ring and add the second muffin half.
7. Close the lid and cook for 3 to 3 ½ minutes.
8. Open carefully and transfer to a plate.
9. Serve and enjoy!

★ Serving Suggestion:Serve with a side of coleslaw.

★ Variation Tip:Add some shredded cheese on top for a cheesier version.

SPICY HORSERADISH BEEF AND CHEESE PANINI

PREPARATION TIME: 15 MINUTES | COOKING TIME: 6 MINUTES | SERVINGS: 4

INGREDIENTS

- 1/3 cup mayonnaise
- 1/4 cup crumbled blue cheese
- 2 teaspoons prepared horseradish
- 1/8 teaspoon pepper
- 1 large sweet onion, thinly sliced
- 1 tablespoon olive oil
- 8 slices white bread
- 8 slices provolone cheese
- 8 slices deli roast beef
- 2 tablespoons butter, softened
- 12 small jalapeno slices

PREPARATION:

1. Combine the mayonnaise, blue cheese, horseradish and pepper in a bowl.
2. Sauté the onions in a skillet on medium heat until they become tender.
3. Spread the bleu cheese mixture on a single side of each piece of bread.
4. Place a layer of cheese, then jalapenos, beef, onions and then a second layer of cheese on half the pieces of bread. Place the other slices of bread on top.

5. Butter the top and bottom of the sandwich and cook the Panini on medium heat for 6 minutes, flipping halfway through. The bread should be brown, and the cheese should be melted.

★ Serving Suggestion: Serve with a side of potato chips.

★ Variation Tip: Use different types of cheese for a varied taste.

 **NUTRITION FACTS:**

Calories: Varies | Total Fats: Varies | Carbs: Varies | Protein: Varies | Fiber: Varies

CORNED BEEF AND CABBAGE PANINI

PREPARATION TIME: 15 MINUTES | **COOKING TIME: 8 MINUTES** | **SERVINGS: 2**

INGREDIENTS

- 1 cup thinly sliced green cabbage
- 1 Tablespoons. olive oil
- ¼ teaspoon. table salt
- Freshly ground black pepper
- 1 teaspoon. yellow mustard seeds
- 2 Tablespoons. unsalted butter, softened
- 4 1/2-inch-thick slices rye bread with caraway seeds
- 1 Tablespoons. grainy mustard, more to taste
- 12 thin slices (6 oz.) corned beef
- 6 thin slices (3 oz.) Muenster cheese
- ¼ cup water

PREPARATION:

1. Mix the water, cabbage, olive oil, mustard seeds, salt, and pepper in a saucepan, heat on medium-high heat until water boils. Once boiling

lower heat to medium-low heat, cover, allow the mixture to cook for 10 to 15 minutes, stirring every once in a while. Remove the cabbage from the saucepan, and set aside any remaining water in the pan.

2. Butter one side of each piece of bread and place mustard on the other side. Top two pieces of bread, mustard side up with corned beef, then cabbage, and finally cheese. Top with the remaining pieces of bread, butter side up.

3. Cook the sandwiches for 6 to 8 minutes on medium heat, and make sure to flip halfway through. The bread should be brown, and the cheese should be melted.

★ Serving Suggestion: Serve with a side of pickles.

★ Variation Tip: Add some sauerkraut for an extra tang.

 **NUTRITION FACTS:**

Calories: Varies | Total Fats: Varies | Carbs: Varies | Protein: Varies | Fiber: Varies

CHEESY BEEF AND EGG SANDWICH

PREPARATION TIME: 5 MINUTES | **COOKING TIME: 4 MINUTES** | **SERVINGS: 1**

INGREDIENTS

- 2 ounces cooked ground Beef
- 2 Bread Slices
- 1 Egg
- 1 ounce shredded Cheddar
- 1 tsp Mayonnaise
- Salt and Pepper, to taste

PREPARATION:

1. Preheat the sandwich maker until the green light appears, and grease it with some cooking spray.

2. Cut the bread slices so they can fit inside the sandwich maker, and place one on top of the bottom ring.

3. Add the beef and cheddar and lower the top ring and cooking plate.

4. Crack the egg into the plate and season it with salt and pepper.

5. Brush the second slices with the mayo and place it with the mayo-side down.

6. Close the lid and cook for 4 minutes.

7. Slide out the cooking plate and open the lid carefully.

8. Tranfer to a plate with a spatula that is not metal.

★ Serving Suggestion:Serve with a side of fresh fruit.

★ Variation Tip:Use different types of cheese for a change in flavor.

★ **NUTRITION FACTS:**

Calories 590 | Total Fats 35g | Carbs 38g | Protein 31g | Fiber 6g

WORCESTERSHIRE BEEF AND CHEDDAR SANDWICH

 PREPARATION TIME: 15 MINUTES   COOKING TIME: 5 MINUTES   SERVINGS: 4

INGREDIENTS

- 1-pound loaf French or Italian-style bread, cut in 4-inch circle
- ¼ cup minced green onions
- 1 tablespoon milk
- ⅛ teaspoon garlic powder
- 1 green bell pepper, sliced in rings
- 1-pound ground beef
- 1 cup sour cream
- 1 teaspoon Worcestershire sauce
- ¾ teaspoon salt
- 2 tablespoons butter, softened
- 2 tomatoes, sliced
- 1 cup shredded Cheddar cheese

PREPARATION:

1. Fry your beef and onions and remove any excess oils.

2. Now add in the following to the mix: pepper, milk, salt, garlic, Worcestershire sauce, garlic, and sour cream.

3. Preheat your Hamilton Beach Breakfast Sandwich Maker.

4. Lift the top cover, ring, and cooking plate.

5. Place one bread slice in the sandwich maker then add ¼ of the butter on top.

6. Now lower the cooking plate and top rings then add ¼ of the rest of the fillings.

7. Place another bread slice on top.

8. Cover the top hood, and let the sandwich cook for 5 minutes.

9. When finished cooking, rotate the handle of the cooking plate clockwise until it stops.

10. Lift the hood, the rings and transfer the sandwich to a plate.

11. Repeat the same steps with remaining ingredients.

★ Serving Suggestion:Serve the sandwich with crispy bacon and your favorite sauce on the side.

★ Variation Tip:You can add a layer of your favorite sauce to the filling as well.

NUTRITION FACTS:

Calories 354; Fat 7.9g; Sodium 704mg; Carbs 6g; Fiber 3.6g; Sugar 6g; Protein 18g

COLESLAW AND CORNED BEEF SANDWICH

PREPARATION TIME: 15 MINUTES   COOKING TIME: 5 MINUTES   SERVINGS: 4

INGREDIENTS

- 8 slices rye bread, cut in 4-inch circle
- 1½ cup deli coleslaw
- 10 ounces deli corned beef (thinly sliced)
- 5 slices deli Swiss cheese
- ⅓cup salad dressing

PREPARATION:

1. Preheat your Hamilton Beach Breakfast sandwich Maker.

2. Lift the top cover, ring, and cooking plate.

3. Place one bread slice in the sandwich maker then top it with ¼ the coleslaw.

4. Now lower the cooking plate and top rings then place ¼ beef, cheese and dressing on top.

5. Add another bread slice on top.

6. Cover the top hood, and let the sandwich cook for 5 minutes.

7. When finished cooking, rotate the handle of the cooking plate clockwise until it stops.

8. Lift the hood, the rings and transfer the sandwich to a plate.

9. Repeat the same steps with remaining ingredients.

★ Serving Suggestion:Serve the sandwich with your favorite sauce on the side.
★ Variation Tip:You can add a lettuce leave to the filling as well.

NUTRITION FACTS:

Calories 354; Fat 7.9g; Sodium 704mg; Carbs 6g; Fiber 3.6g; Sugar 6g; Protein 18g

CLASSIC BEEF CHEESE BURGER

PREPARATION TIME: 15 MINUTES   COOKING TIME: 10 MINUTES   SERVINGS: 1

INGREDIENTS

- 200 grams ground beef
- 1 hamburger bun
- 1 slice of cheese
- 2 lettuce leaves
- 1 slice of tomato
- Appropriate amount of onion rings
- Appropriate amount of salt, black pepper, soy sauce, cooking wine, starch

PREPARATION:

1. Add salt, black pepper, soy sauce, cooking wine and starch to the ground beef, stir evenly to make the patty.

2. Brush a little oil in the Hamilton Beach breakfast sandwich maker, and put in the patty to fry until cooked.

3. Cut the hamburger bun, and lay lettuce leaves, tomato slices, fried beef patty and cheese in sequence at the bottom.

4. Cover with the top of the hamburger bun.

 **NUTRITION FACTS:**

Calories: 550 | Fat: 25g | Sodium: 700mg | Carbs: 45g | Fiber: 3g | Sugar: 8g | Protein: 30g

GARLIC BEEF SANDWICHES

PREPARATION TIME: 15 MINUTES | COOKING TIME: 5 MINUTES | SERVINGS: 3

INGREDIENTS

- 1 tablespoon vegetable oil
- 1 ½ pound boneless beef sirloin steak, sliced
- 1 onion, sliced
- 3 garlic cloves, minced
- 3 large celery ribs, sliced
- 3 tablespoons minced fresh ginger root
- 2 tablespoons soy sauce
- 1 teaspoon chili oil
- 6 English muffins, split

PREPARATION:

1. In a large skillet; heat vegetable oil on medium-high heat

2. Then, stir in sirloin strips and sauté a few minutes until the strips starts to brown.

3. Next, stir in onion and garlic; sauté for about 2 minutes.

4. Add in the celery and ginger, keep on cooking for about 3 minutes or until the onion has softened.

5. Now, season it with soy sauce and chili oil.

6. Preheat your Hamilton Beach Breakfast Sandwich Maker.

7. Place the lower half of the muffin in the sandwich maker.

8. Now lower the cooking plate and top rings then add⅓of the fillings.

9. Add the other top half of the muffin on top.

10. Cover the top hood, and let the sandwich cook for 5 minutes.

11. When finished cooking, rotate the handle of the cooking plate clockwise until it stops.

12. Lift the hood, the rings and transfer the sandwich to a plate.

13. Repeat the same steps with remaining ingredients.

 **NUTRITION FACTS:**

Calories 275 | Fat 1.4g | Sodium 582mg | Carbs 31.5g | Fiber 1.1g | Sugar 0.1g | Protein 29.8g

ROASTED BEEF AND PROVOLONE MUFFIN SANDWICH

PREPARATION TIME: 15 MINUTES | COOKING TIME: 5 MINUTES | SERVINGS: 4

INGREDIENTS

- 1 (10.5 ounces) can beef consommé
- 1 cup water
- 1 pound sliced deli roast beef
- 8 slices provolone cheese
- 4 English muffins, split

PREPARATION:

1. Open your buns and place them in a casserole dish.

2. Now combine water and beef consommé in a pan to make a broth.

3. Cook your beef in this mixture for 5 minutes.

4. Preheat your Hamilton Beach Breakfast Sandwich Maker.

5. Lift the top cover, ring, and cooking plate.

6. Place the lower half of the muffin in the sandwich maker.

7. Now lower the cooking plate and top rings, then add ¼ of the beef and cheese on top.

8. Add the other top half of the muffin on top.

9. Cover the top hood, and let the sandwich cook for 5 minutes.

10. When finished cooking, rotate the handle of the cooking plate clockwise until it stops.

11. Lift the hood, the rings and transfer the sandwich to a plate.

12. Repeat the same steps with remaining ingredients.

★ Serving Suggestion:Serve the sandwich with crispy bacon and your favorite sauce on the side.
★ Variation Tip:You can add a lettuce leave to the filling as well.

 **NUTRITION FACTS:**

Calories 380 | Fat 29g | Sodium 821mg | Carbs 34.6g | Fiber 0g | Sugar 0g | Protein 30g

SPICY BEEF BURGER

PREPARATION TIME: 18 MINUTES | COOKING TIME: 12 MINUTES | SERVINGS: 1

INGREDIENTS

- 250 grams ground beef
- 1 hamburger bun
- 2 slices of Mexican chili peppers
- 1 slice of cheddar cheese
- 2 slices of pickled cucumbers
- Appropriate amount of mayonnaise, chili sauce
- Appropriate amount of salt, black pepper, cumin powder

PREPARATION:

1. Add salt, black pepper and cumin powder to the ground beef, stir evenly to make the patty.

2. Preheat the sandwich maker, brush oil, and put in the patty to fry until fully cooked.

3. Cut the hamburger bun in the middle, and smear mayonnaise and chili sauce.

4. Put in pickled cucumber slices, beef patty, Mexican chili pepper slices and cheddar cheese in sequence, and cover with the top of the bun.

★ Serving Suggestion:Serve with a side of sweet potato fries or a small salad.
★ Variation Tip:You can add some sliced jalapenos for an extra spicy kick.

NUTRITION FACTS:

Calories: 600 | Fat: 28g | Sodium: 800mg | Carbs: 48g | Fiber: 3g | Sugar: 9g | Protein: 32g

MUSHROOM BEEF BURGER

PREPARATION TIME: 16 MINUTES | COOKING TIME: 11 MINUTES | SERVINGS: 1 | PREPARATION TIME: 5 MINUTES | COOKING TIME: 4 MINUTES | SERVINGS: 1

INGREDIENTS

- 180 grams ground beef
- 1 hamburger bun
- 50 grams mushrooms (sliced)
- 1 slice of Swiss cheese
- Appropriate amount of ketchup
- Appropriate amount of salt, black pepper, olive oil

PREPARATION:

1. Add salt and black pepper to the ground beef and stir evenly to make the patty.

2. Pour olive oil into the pan, put in the mushroom slices and fry until cooked, then set aside.

3. Fry the beef patty until golden on both sides in the sandwich maker.

4. Cut the hamburger bun, smear ketchup at the bottom, put the beef patty, mushroom slices and Swiss cheese on it, and cover with the top of the bun.

★ Serving Suggestion:Serve with a side of onion rings or a small cup of coleslaw.

★ Variation Tip:You can add some sautéed onions or a slice of bacon for extra flavor.

NUTRITION FACTS:

Calories: 500 | Fat: 20g | Sodium: 650mg | Carbs: 40g | Fiber: 2g | Sugar: 7g | Protein: 28g

PULLED PORK SANDWICH

INGREDIENTS

- 1 smaller Hamburger Bun
- 3 ounces Pulled Pork
- 4 Red Onion Rings
- ½ Pickle, sliced
- 2 tsp Mustard

PREPARATION:

1. Preheat the sandwich maker and grease it with some cooking spray.

2. Cut the bun in half and spread the insides with the mustard.

3. When the green light appears, place one bun half into the bottom ring with the cut-side up.

4. Top with pork, onion rings, and pickle.

5. Lower the top ring and plate and place the second bun half inside.

6. Close and cook for 4 minutes.

7. Rotate clockwise and open carefully.

8. Serve and enjoy!

★ Serving Suggestion:Serve with a side of coleslaw.

★ Variation Tip:Add some barbecue sauce for a sweeter flavor.

NUTRITION FACTS:

Calories 372 | Total Fats 18g | Carbs 27g | Protein 27g | Fiber 2.2g

ROASTED BEEF AND PROVOLONE MUFFIN SANDWICH

PREPARATION TIME: 15 MINUTES   COOKING TIME: 5 MINUTES   SERVINGS: 4

INGREDIENTS

- 1 (10.5 ounces) can beef consommé
- 1 cup water
- 1 pound sliced deli roast beef
- 8 slices provolone cheese
- 4 English muffins, split

PREPARATION:

1. Open your buns and place them in a casserole dish.

2. Now combine water and beef consommé in a pan to make a broth.

3. Cook your beef in this mixture for 5 minutes.

4. Preheat your Hamilton Beach Breakfast Sandwich Maker.

5. Lift the top cover, ring, and cooking plate.

6. Place the lower half of the muffin in the sandwich maker.

7. Now lower the cooking plate and top rings, then add ¼ of the beef and cheese on top.

8. Add the other top half of the muffin on top.

9. Cover the top hood, and let the sandwich cook for 5 minutes.

10. When finished cooking, rotate the handle of the cooking plate clockwise until it stops.

11. Lift the hood, the rings and transfer the sandwich to a plate.

12. Repeat the same steps with remaining ingredients.

★ Serving Suggestion:Serve the sandwich with crispy bacon and your favorite sauce on the side.
★ Variation Tip:You can add a lettuce leave to the filling as well.

 **NUTRITION FACTS:**

Calories 380 | Fat 29g | Sodium 821mg | Carbs 34.6g | Fiber 0g | Sugar 0g | Protein 30g

HERBED BEEF AND GIARDINIERA SANDWICH

PREPARATION TIME: 15 MINUTES   COOKING TIME: 1 HR. 35 MINUTES   SERVINGS: 4

INGREDIENTS

- 1½ lbs. boneless beef chuck, cut into 2-inch pieces
- Salt and black pepper to taste
- 1 tablespoon vegetable oil
- 6 garlic cloves, sliced
- 2 tablespoons white vinegar
- 1 tablespoon dried oregano
- 1½ teaspoons salt
- 1 teaspoon dried thyme
- 1 teaspoon dried rosemary
- 1 teaspoon black pepper
- 1 bay leaf
- ¼ teaspoon red pepper flakes
- 3 cups chicken broth
- 4 hamburger buns, sliced in half
- 1 cup chopped giardiniera (pickled Italian vegetables)
- 2 teaspoons chopped fresh flat-leaf parsley

PREPARATION:

1. Sear beef with black pepper, salt and oil in a deep skillet for 8 minutes until brown.

2. Stir in chicken broth, red pepper flakes, bay leaf, black pepper, rosemary, thyme, salt, oregano, vinegar and garlic..

3. Cover and cook on a simmer for 1 ½ hours.

4. Strain and shred the cooked meat with a fork.

5. Place half of a bun, cut-side up, inside the bottom tray of the sandwich maker.

6. Now lower the cooking plate and top rings then place ¼ beef and other ingredients on top.

7. Place the other top half of the bun on top.

8. Cover the top hood, and let the sandwich cook for 5 minutes.

9. Rotate the handle of the cooking plate clockwise until it stops.

10. Lift the hood, the rings and transfer the sandwich to a plate.

11. Repeat the same with the remaining ingredients.

★ Serving Suggestion:Serve the sandwich with a broccoli salad on the side.

★ Variation Tip:Enjoy sautéed veggies on the side for a change of taste.

NUTRITION FACTS:

Calories 382 | Fat 4g |Sodium 232mg | Carbs 4g | Fiber 1g | Sugar 0g | Protein 21g

BEEF AND FRIED MUSHROOM SANDWICH

PREPARATION TIME: 15 MINUTES

COOKING TIME: 5 MINUTES

SERVINGS: 4

INGREDIENTS

- 1 loaf hearty country bread, cut in 4-inch circle
- 3 tablespoon vegetable oil
- 3-pound boneless beef round steak, 2 inches thick
- 1 onion, sliced

- 2 cup sliced fresh mushrooms
- 1 garlic clove, minced
- Salt to taste
- Ground black pepper to taste
- Garlic salt to taste

PREPARATION:

1. Fry your steak in 1 tablespoon of veggie oil for 6 minutes per side then place the steak to the side.

2. Stir fry your mushrooms, onions, and garlic for 7 minutes until the onions are see through in 2 more tablespoons of veggie oil.

3. Preheat your Hamilton Beach Breakfast Sandwich Maker.

4. Lift the top cover, ring, and cooking plate.

5. Place one bread slice in the sandwich maker then add butter on top.

6. Now lower the cooking plate and top rings then add ¼ of the rest of the fillings.

7. Place another bread slice on top.

8. Cover the top hood, and let the sandwich cook for 5 minutes.

9. When finished cooking, rotate the handle of the cooking plate clockwise until it stops.

10. Lift the hood, the rings and transfer the sandwich to a plate.

11. Repeat the same steps with remaining ingredients.

★ Serving Suggestion:Serve the sandwich with your favorite sauce on the side.

★ Variation Tip:Add some additional dried herbs to the filling.

NUTRITION FACTS:

Calories 305 | Fat 15g | Sodium 482mg | Carbs 17g | Fiber 3g

BEEF AND CARROT SANDWICH

PREPARATION TIME: 15 MINUTES | COOKING TIME: 5 MINUTES | SERVINGS: 2

INGREDIENTS

- 1 cup chopped cooked beef
- 2 stalks celery, chopped
- 1 carrot, diced
- ¼ cup chopped onion
- 3 tablespoons mayonnaise
- ¼ teaspoons salt
- ⅛ teaspoons ground black pepper
- ⅛ teaspoons garlic powder
- 2 sesame seed buns, toasted until the broiler
- 2 eggs

PREPARATION:

1. Get a bowl, combine: garlic powder, beef, black pepper, celery, salt, carrot, mayo, and onion. Stir the mix until it is even.

2. Preheat your Hamilton Beach Breakfast Sandwich Maker.

3. Lift the top cover, ring, and cooking plate.

4. Place the lower half of the muffin in the sandwich maker and top with ½ of the remaining fillings.

5. Now lower the cooking plate and top rings, then pour in ½ of the egg.

6. Add another bun half on top.

7. Cover the top hood, and let the sandwich cook for 5 minutes.

8. When finished cooking, rotate the handle of the cooking plate clockwise until it stops.

9. Lift the hood, the rings and transfer the sandwich to a plate.

10. Repeat the same steps with remaining ingredients.

11. Enjoy on toasted sesame seed buns.

★ Serving Suggestion: Serve the sandwich with coleslaw and your favorite sauce on the side.
★ Variation Tip:Add some additional ground black pepper to the filling.

 **NUTRITION FACTS:**

Calories 308 | Fat 24g |Sodium 715mg | Carbs 0.8g | Fiber 0.1g | Sugar 0.1g | Protein 21.9g

PORK AND EGG TORTILLA OPEN SANDWICH

PREPARATION TIME: 5 MINUTES | COOKING TIME: 4 MINUTES | SERVINGS: 4

INGREDIENTS

- 1 Wheat Tortilla
- 1 Egg
- 2 ounces cooked ground Pork
- 1 ounce shredded Cheddar Cheese
- 1 tbsp chopped Red Onion
- 1 tbsp Salsa

PREPARATION:

1. Preheat and grease the sandwich maker.

2. Cut the tortilla, if needed, to fit inside the sandwich maker, and then add it to the bottom ring.

3. Place the pork on top of it, sprinkle the cheddar over, and top with the onion.

4. Lower the top ring and crack the egg into it.

5. Close the unit and wait for about 4 minutes before rotating the handle clockwise.

6. Open and transfer to a plate carefully.

7. Top with the salsa.

8. Enjoy!

★ Serving Suggestion:Serve with a side of guacamole.

★ Variation Tip:Replace the salsa with sour cream for a creamier taste.

 **NUTRITION FACTS:**

Calories 466 | Total Fats 28.3g | Carbs 20.5g | Protein 31g | Fiber 1.5g

HOT PORK SAUSAGE AND SCRAMBLED EGG SANDWICH

PREPARATION TIME: 5 MINUTES | COOKING TIME: 4 MINUTES | SERVINGS: 1

INGREDIENTS

- 2 ounces ground Pork Sausage, cooked
- 1 ounce shredded Cheddar Cheese
- 1 Egg
- ¼ tsp dried Thyme
- 1 Biscuit
- ½ tsp Hot Pepper Sauce
- Salt and Pepper, to taste

PREPARATION:

1. Preheat and grease the sandwich maker with cooking spray.

2. Cut the biscuit in half and place one half inside the bottom ring.

3. Top with the sausage and cheddar, and sprinkle the hot sauce over.

4. Lower the top ring and cooking plate, and crack the egg into it.

5. Season with salt and pepper and sprinkle the thyme over.

6. Close the unit and wait 4 minutes before rotating clockwise to open.

7. Serve and enjoy!

★ Serving Suggestion:Serve with a side of fresh fruit.

★ Variation Tip: Add some sliced mushrooms for an extra flavor.

 **NUTRITION FACTS:**

Calories 455 | Total Fats 33g | Carbs 13g | Protein 26g | Fiber 0.4g

PORK MUFFIN SANDWICH

PREPARATION TIME: 5 MINUTES | COOKING TIME: 5 MINUTES | SERVINGS: 1

INGREDIENTS

- 1 Frozen Pork Pattie
- 1 English Muffin
- 1 Slice Cheddar Cheese
- 1 tsp Dijon Mustard

PREPARATION:

1. Preheat and grease the sandwich maker.

2. Cut the muffin in half and brush one of the halves with the mustard.

. Place the muffin half onto the bottom ring with he mustard-side up.

4. Top with the frozen pattie and place the heese on top.

5. Lower the top ring and add the second half ith the cut-side down.

5. Cook for full 5 minutes.

7. Open by rotating clockwise and lifting the lid. ransfer to a plate and enjoy

★ Serving Suggestion:Serve with a side of apple slices.

★ Variation Tip:Use a different type of cheese for a change.

NUTRITION FACTS:

Calories 490 | Total Fats 27g | Carbs 25g | Protein 33g | Fiber 2g

VEGGIE AND PORK MAYO SANDWICH

 PREPARATION TIME: 5 MINUTES

 COOKING TIME: 3 MINUTES   SERVINGS: 1

INGREDIENTS

- 1 smaller Hamburger Bun
- 1 tbsp shredded Carrots
- 1 tbsp shredded Cabbage
- 1 tbsp chopped Onion
- 1 tsp Pickle Relish
- 1 tbsp Mayonnaise
- 2 ounces chopped cooked Pork
- Salt and Pepper, to taste

PREPARATION:

1. Grease the Hamilton Beach Breakfast Sandwich Maker with cooking spray and preheat t.

2. Cut the hamburger bun in half and brush the mayonnaise over the insides of the bun.

3. Place one of the halves inside the bottom ring, with the cut-side up.

4. Top with the pork and veggies.

5. Season with salt and pepper, and top with the pickle relish.

6. Lower the top ring and add the second half of the bun with the cut-side down.

7. Close the unit and cook for 3 ½ minutes.

8. Rotate the handle clockwise to open.

9. Transfer to a plate and enjoy!

★ Serving Suggestion:Serve with a side of potato chips.

★ Variation Tip:Add some sliced tomatoes for extra freshness.

NUTRITION FACTS:

Calories 395 | Total Fats 25g | Carbs 28g | Protein 20g | Fiber 1.5g

SPICY PORK AND PIMENTO SANDWICH

 PREPARATION TIME: 5 MINUTES

 COOKING TIME: 4 MINUTES   SERVINGS: 1

INGREDIENTS

- 3 ounces cooked ground Pork
- 1 ounce shredded Pimento Cheese
- 1 tbsp chopped Red Onion
- 1 smaller Hamburger Bun
- 1 ½ tsp Tomato Puree
- ½ tsp Chili Powder

PREPARATION:

1. Preheat the sandwich maker and grease it with some cooking spray.

2. Cut the bun in half.

3. When the green light appears, add half of the bun to the bottom ring.

4. Then, place the pork, red onion, and cheese on top.

5. Sprinkle the chili powder over.

6. Lower the top ring and cooking plate.

7. Top the sandwich with the second half with the cut-side down.

8. Close and cook for 4 minutes.

9. Finally, slide out clockwise, lift it open, and transfer to a plate with a spatula that's not metal.

10. Serve and enjoy!

★ Serving Suggestion:Serve with a side of pickled jalapenos.

★ Variation Tip:Add a slice of avocado for a creamier texture.

NUTRITION FACTS:

Calories 532 | Total Fats 28.5g | Carbs 34.4g | Protein 33g | Fiber 1.2g

MAYO GOURMET PORK SANDWICH

🏅 PREPARATION TIME: 15 MINUTES   🏅 COOKING TIME: 5 MINUTES   🏅 SERVINGS: 1

INGREDIENTS

- Choice of greens
- 3 tablespoons mayonnaise
- ⅛ piece red bell pepper, sliced
- 2 sliced Gardenia loaf bread, cut in 4-inch circle
- 4 pounds pork strips

PREPARATION:

1. Cook pork strips and bell peppers in a skillet until tender.

2. Preheat your Hamilton Beach Breakfast Sandwich Maker.

3. Lift the top cover, ring, and cooking plate.

4. Place one bread slice in the sandwich maker and spread mayonnaise on top.

5. Now lower the cooking plate and top rings then place ¼ cup pork, peppers and greens on top.

6. Add another bread slice on top.

7. Cover the top hood, and let the sandwich cook for 5 minutes.

8. When finished cooking, rotate the handle of the cooking plate clockwise until it stops.

9. Lift the hood, the rings and transfer the sandwich to a plate.

10. Repeat the same steps with remaining ingredients.

★ Serving Suggestion:Serve the sandwich with crispy bacon and your favorite sauce on the side.

★ Variation Tip:You can add a drizzle of paprika on top of the filling as well.

NUTRITION FACTS:

Calories 336 | Fat 6g |Sodium 181mg | Carbs 1.3g | Fiber 0.2g | Sugar 0.4g | Protein 69.2g

HERBED CAULIFLOWER AND PORK SANDWICH

INGREDIENTS

- 1 head cauliflower, riced and cooked
- 1 egg, beaten
- 1 ½ cups cheddar cheese, grated
- 12 slices mozzarella cheese
- ⅛ teaspoon dried sage
- ⅛ teaspoon dried oregano
- Dash of ground mustard seed
- Dash of dried thyme
- Ground black pepper, to taste
- 1 cup pulled barbecue pork
- Butter, for greasing
- Fresh parsley, for garnish

PREPARATION:

1. Preheat your oven to 350°F.

2. In a blender, combine the cooked cauliflower, beaten egg, grated cheese, dried herbs, and spices. Blend until you achieve a smooth consistency.

3. Line a baking sheet with parchment paper and portion the cauliflower mixture into equal rounds, about 3-4 inches in diameter, on the sheet.

4. Bake the cauliflower rounds for about 5 minutes on each side.

5. Preheat your Hamilton Beach Breakfast Sandwich Maker.

6. Lift the top cover, ring, and cooking plate.

7. Place one cauliflower round in the sandwich maker and layer with pulled pork.

8. Add a slice of mozzarella cheese on top.

9. Lower the cooking plate and top rings.

10. Place the second cauliflower round on top and brush with butter.

11. Close the top hood and cook the sandwich for about 5 minutes.

12. Once cooking is complete, rotate the cooking plate handle clockwise until it stops.

13. Lift the hood and rings, then transfer the sandwich to a plate.

14. Repeat the process with the remaining ingredients.

15. Garnish with fresh parsley and serve.

★ Serving Suggestion: Pair the sandwich with coleslaw and your favorite sauce on the side.
★ Variation Tip: You can also add a lettuce leaf to the filling.

 **NUTRITION FACTS:**

Calories: 195 | Fat: 3g | Sodium: 355mg | Carbs: 7.7g | Fiber: 1g | Sugar: 25g | Protein: 1g

APPLE AND PORK MUFFIN MELL

INGREDIENTS

- 2 ounces cooked Pork, chopped
- 2 slices Granny Smith Apple
- 1 English Muffin
- 1 tbsp Cream Cheese
- 1 ounce shredded Cheese by choice

PREPARATION:

1. First, preheat and grease the sandwich maker with cooking spray.

2. Second, cut the muffin in half and spread the cream cheese over its insides.

3. Then, place one half on top of the bottom ring, with the cream cheese side up.

4. After that, arrange the apple slices on top.

5. Next, add the pork and top with the cheese.

6. Now, lower the top ring and cooking plate and place the second half with the cut-side down.

7. Then, close and cook for 4 minutes.

8. Next, slide out the plate and rotate clockwise.

9. Finally, transfer to a plate and enjoy!

★ Serving Suggestion:Serve with a side of fresh fruit.

★ Variation Tip:Add some honey for a sweeter taste.

 **NUTRITION FACTS:**

Calories 471 |Total Fats 27g |Carbs 29g |Protein 28g |Fiber: 2.5g

PAN-FRIED PORK SANDWICH

PREPARATION TIME: 5 MINUTES | COOKING TIME: 4 MINUTES | SERVINGS: 1

INGREDIENTS

- 200 grams of pork loin
- 2 slices of whole wheat bread
- 2 lettuce leaves
- 1 slice tomato
- Mayonnaise in moderation
- Salt, black pepper, light soy sauce to taste

PREPARATION:

1. First, thinly slice the pork tenderloin and marinate briefly with salt, black pepper and light soy sauce.

2. Next, brush a little oil in a sandwich maker and fry the pork tenderloin until golden on both sides.

3. Then, cut the whole wheat bread, spread mayonnaise on the bottom, top with lettuce leaves, tomato slices and fried pork.

4. Finally, cover the top slice of bread.

5. Serve and enjoy.

★ Serving Suggestion:Serve with a side of potato chips.

★ Variation Tip:Add some sliced cucumbers for extra crunch.

 **NUTRITION FACTS:**

Calories: 450 | Fat: 18g | Sodium: 650mg | Carbs: 40g | Fiber: 5g | Sugar: 8g | Protein: 30g

SALMON AND PISTACHIO SANDWICH

 PREPARATION TIME: 5 MINUTES

 COOKING TIME: 4 MINUTES

 SERVINGS: 1

INGREDIENTS

- 2 Bread Slices
- 2 ounces chopped cooked Salmon
- 2 tsp chopped Pistachios
- 1 ounce shredded Mozzarella

PREPARATION:

1. Preheat and grease the sandwich maker with cooking spray.
2. Cut the bread slices into circles so they can fit perfectly inside the unit.
3. Add the first slice to the bottom ring and place the salmon on top.
4. Add the pistachios over and top with the mozzarella.
5. Lower the top ring and add the remaining bread slice.
6. Close and cook for 3 – 4 minutes.
7. Rotate clockwise and lift open.
8. Transfer to a plate and enjoy!

★ Serving Suggestion: Serve the sandwich with coleslaw and your favorite sauce on the side.
★ Variation Tip: Add some additional ground black pepper to the filling.

 **NUTRITION FACTS:**

Calories 423| Total Fats 16g| Carbs 41g| Protein 30.8g | Fiber: 7g

---

AWESOME SALMON BURGERS WITH HARISSA MAYO

 PREPARATION TIME: 15 MINUTES

 COOKING TIME: 11 MINUTES

 SERVINGS: 6

INGREDIENTS

- Cumber relish
- 1 English cucumber, sliced
- ⅓ cup rice vinegar
- 1 tablespoon chopped dill
- 1 shallot, minced
- 1 teaspoon sugar
- 1 teaspoon kosher salt

Harissa mayo

- ⅔ cup mayonnaise
- ¼ cup Greek yoghurt
- 2 tablespoons harissa
- 1 teaspoon grated lemon zest
- 1 tablespoon fresh lemon juice
- Kosher salt, to taste
- Black pepper, to taste

Salmon burgers

- 5 scallions, chopped
- 1 small red bell pepper, chopped
- 1 small green bell pepper, chopped
- 1 ½ lbs. skinless center-cut salmon fillet, cut into cubes
- 1/2 cup plain dry breadcrumbs
- 1 tablespoon kosher salt
- ½ teaspoon black pepper

To cook:
- 2 tablespoons unsalted butter
- ¼ cup olive oil
- 6 brioche buns, split
- Lettuce and tomato slices, for serving

PREPARATION:

1. Blend all the ingredients for salmon burgers in a food processor for 1 minute.

2. Mix harissa mayo ingredients in a suitable bowl.

3. Whisk the cucumber relish ingredients in another bowl.

4. Set a pan with oil over medium heat.

5. Make 6 patties out of the salmon mixture and sear them in the oil for 3 minutes per side.

6. Preheat your Hamilton Beach Breakfast Sandwich Maker until PREHEAT light gets green.

7. Lift the top cover, ring, and cooking plate.

8. Place half of a bun cut-side up, inside the bottom tray of the sandwich maker.

9. Add ⅙ of the harissa mayo, 1 salmon patty and ⅙ of the cucumber relish on top.

10. Now lower the cooking plate and top rings.

11. Place the other top half of the bun on top.

12. Cover the top hood, and let the sandwich cook for 5 minutes.

13. Rotate the handle of the cooking plate clockwise until it stops.

14. Lift the hood, the rings and transfer the sandwich to a plate.

15. Repeat the same steps with the remaining ingredients.

16. Serve with the lettuce and tomato slices.

★ Serving Suggestion: Serve the sandwich with crispy bacon and your favorite sauce on the side.

★ Variation Tip: Add a layer of pickled onions for a change of taste.

NUTRITION FACTS:

Calories 425 | Fat 14g | Sodium 411mg | Carbs 24g | Fiber 0.3g | Sugar 1g | Protein 28.3g

CRAB CAKE AND BISCUIT SANDWICH

PREPARATION TIME: 5 MINUTES | COOKING TIME: 3 MINUTES | SERVINGS: 1

INGREDIENTS
- 1 frozen Crab Cake Pattie
- 2 tsp Sour Cream
- 1 slice American Cheese
- ½ Pickle, sliced
- 1 Biscuit

PREPARATION:

1. Preheat the sandwich maker and grease it with some cooking spray.

2. Cut the biscuit in half and place one half to the bottom ring of the unit.

3. Spread half of the sour cream over and add the crab cake on top.

4. Spread the remaining sour cream over the crab cake, arrange the pickle slices over, and top with the cheese.

5. Lower the top ring and add the second biscuit half.

6. Close the unit and cook for 3 ½ minutes.

7. Open carefully and transfer to a plate.

8. Serve and enjoy!

★ Serving Suggestion: Serve with a side of potato chips for added crunch.

★ Variation Tip: Add some slices of tomato for an extra flavor boost.

TUNA AND CORN MUFFIN SANDWICH

NUTRITIOUS SALMON BACON SANDWICH

 PREPARATION TIME: 5 MINUTES   COOKING TIME: 3 MINUTES   SERVINGS: 1

 PREPARATION TIME: 5 MINUTES COOKING TIME: 3 MINUTES SERVINGS: 1

INGREDIENTS

- 1 Whole Wheat English Muffin
- 2 ounces canned Tuna, drained
- 2 tsp Mayonnaise
- 2 tsp canned Corn
- 2 tsp chopped Tomatoes

PREPARATION:

1. Preheat and grease the unit.
2. Cut the English muffin half.
3. When the green light appears, add half of the muffin to the bottom ring.
4. Combine together the tuna, mayonnaise, tomatoes, and corn.
5. Place the tuna mixture on top of the muffin half.
6. Lower the top ring and add the second half of the muffin.
7. Close the unit and cook for 3 minutes.
8. Rotate clockwise and open. Transfer to a plate.
9. Serve and enjoy!

★ Serving Suggestion: For the tuna and corn muffin sandwich, pair with a fresh fruit salad.
★ Variation Tip: For the tuna and corn muffin sandwich, substitute the mayonnaise with Greek yogurt for a healthier option.

INGREDIENTS

- 2 ounces canned Salmon
- 1 Bacon Slice, cooked
- 2 Bread Slices
- 1 ounce shredded Mozzarella Cheese
- 1 tsp Pickle Relish
- ½ Pickle, sliced
- 1 tsp Dijon Mustard
- 1 tsp Tomato Puree

PREPARATION:

1. Preheat the sandwich maker and grease it with some cooking spray.
2. Cut the bread slices so they can fit the unit.
3. Brush one of the bread slices with Dijon mustard and place it on top of the bottom ring, with the mustard-side up.
4. Add the salmon and bacon on top and sprinkle with the relish and tomato puree.
5. Arrange the pickle slices over and top with the mozzarella.
6. Lower the top ring and add the second bread slice.
7. Cover the unit and cook for about 3 – 4 minutes.
8. Rotate clockwise to open and transfer to a plate.
9. Serve and enjoy!

NUTRITION FACTS:

Calories: 420 Total Fats: 34g Carbs: 25g Protein: 28g Fiber: 3.5g

SNAPPER CHEESE ENERGY SANDWICH

PREPARATION TIME: 5 MINUTES | COOKING TIME: 3 MINUTES | SERVINGS: 1

INGREDIENTS

- 2 Bread Slices
- 2 ounces chopped cooked Tilapia Fillet
- 1 slice Pimento Cheese
- 2 tsp Dijon Mustard
- ¼ tsp chopped Parsley

PREPARATION:

1. Preheat the sandwich maker and apply some cooking spray to grease it.

2. Cut the bread slices to a size that fits inside the unit, and spread the Dijon over them.

3. Place one bread slice in the bottom ring, with the mustard side facing upwards.

4. Add the tilapia, sprinkle with parsley, and cover with cheese.

5. Lower the ring and add the second bread slice, with the mustard side facing downwards.

6. Close the device and cook for 3 to 4 minutes.

7. Open it carefully and transfer to a plate.

8. Serve and enjoy!

★ Serving Suggestion: Serve with a side of fresh fruit salad.

★ Variation Tip: Add some sliced onions for an enhanced flavor.

NUTRITION FACTS:

Calories 388 Total Fats 13g Carbs 35g Protein 29g Fiber: 6g

NUTRITIOUS FISH FINGER VITALITY MEAL

PREPARATION TIME: 5 MINUTES | COOKING TIME: 3 MINUTES | SERVINGS: 1

INGREDIENTS

- 2 Fish Fingers, cooked and chopped
- 1 small Hamburger Bun
- 1 tbsp Cream Cheese
- 1 ounce Cheddar Cheese
- 1 tbsp chopped Red Onion

PREPARATION:

1. Preheat the sandwich maker and apply some cooking spray to grease it.

2. Cut the bun in half and spread the cream cheese on it.

3. Place one half on the bottom ring, with the cream cheese side facing up.

4. Add the pieces of fish fingers on top, sprinkle with the red onion and cover with the cheddar.

5. Lower the cooking plate and top ring and add the second half of the bun, with the cream cheese facing down.

6. Close the unit and cook for approximately 4 minutes.

7. Open it carefully and transfer to a plate.

8. Serve and enjoy!

★ Serving Suggestion: Serve with a side of potato wedges.

★ Variation Tip: Add some slices of cucumber for a refreshing twist.

NUTRITION FACTS:

Calories 350 Total Fats 20g Carbs 26g Protein 22g Fiber: 4g

TENDER COD PITA SANDWICH

PREPARATION TIME: 5 MINUTES | COOKING TIME: 3 MINUTES | SERVINGS: 1

INGREDIENTS

- 1 small Pita Bread, about 4 inches
- 3 ounces cooked Cod, chopped
- 1 tbsp Greek Yogurt
- 1 tsp chopped Dill
- ¼ tsp Garlic Powder
- 1 ounce shredded Cheddar Cheese

PREPARATION:

1. Preheat the unit until the green light appears. Grease with cooking spray.
2. Add the pita bread to the bottom ring and place the cod on top.
3. Sprinkle with the garlic powder and top with the cheddar.
4. Close the lid and cook for 3 minutes or so.
5. Combine the yogurt and dill.
6. Open the lid carefully and transfer to a plate.
7. Drizzle the yogurt and dill mixture over.
8. Enjoy!

★ Serving Suggestion:Serve with a side of cucumber slices.

★ Variation Tip:Add some sliced tomatoes for extra flavor.

 **NUTRITION FACTS:**

Calories: 282 Total Fats: 12g Carbs: 17g Protein: 26.5g Fiber: 0.6g

---

DELICIOUS SHRIMP BISCUIT SANDWICH

PREPARATION TIME: 5 MINUTES | COOKING TIME: 3 MINUTES | SERVINGS: 1

INGREDIENTS

- 4 small Shrimp, cooked
- ½ tbsp Salsa
- 2 tsp Cream Cheese
- 1 ounce shredded Mozzarella Cheese
- 1 Biscuit

PREPARATION:

1. Preheat the sandwich maker and grease it with some cooking spray.
2. Cut the biscuit in half and spread the cream cheese over the insides.
3. Add one half of the biscuit to the bottom ring, with the cream cheese up.
4. Top with the shrimp and salsa, and sprinkle the mozzarella cheese over.
5. Lower the top ring and add the second biscuit half, with the cream cheese down.
6. Close the unit and cook for 3 minutes.
7. Rotate clockwise and open carefully.
8. Serve and enjoy!

★ Serving Suggestion:Serve with a side of carrot sticks.

★ Variation Tip:Add some chopped scallions for extra flavor.

 **NUTRITION FACTS:**

Calories: 222 Total Fats: 11g Carbs: 13g Protein: 19g Fiber: 0.5g

VIBRANT SHRIMP PAN BURGER

PREPARATION TIME: 15 MINUTES | COOKING TIME: 11 MINUTES | SERVINGS: 4

INGREDIENTS

- 5 tablespoons unsalted butter
- 1 lb. peeled and deveined large shrimp, chopped
- 1 large egg
- ¾ cup panko
- ¼ cup scallions, chopped
- 1 ½ teaspoon salt
- ¾ teaspoon old bay seasoning
- ½ teaspoon lemon zest
- 1 ½ tablespoon fresh lemon juice
- ½ cup mayonnaise
- 1 tablespoon whole-grain mustard
- 1 teaspoon Mexican-style hot sauce
- 4 sesame seed hamburger buns, split
- 1 cup shredded iceberg lettuce
- 1 small tomato, sliced
- 1 ripe medium-size avocado, sliced

PREPARATION:

1. First, mix mayonnaise with salt, mustard, hot sauce, old bay seasoning and scallion in a bowl.

2. Next, dip the shrimp in the egg then in panko crumbs.

3. Then, melt butter in a skillet and sear the shrimp for 2 – 3 minutes per side until golden brown. Fry all the coated shrimp and transfer them to a plate.

4. Preheat your Hamilton Beach Breakfast Sandwich Maker until PREHEAT light gets green. Lift the top cover, ring, and cooking plate.

5. Place half of a bun, cut-side up, inside the bottom tray of the sandwich maker.

6. Arrange a lettuce leaf on top of the bun then add ¼ of the mayonnaise on top.

7. Now lower the cooking plate and top rings, place ¼ of the shrimp, tomato, avocado and lettuce on top.

8. Place the other top half of the bun on top.

9. Cover the top hood, and let the sandwich cook for 5 minutes.

10. Rotate the handle of the cooking plate clockwise until it stops.

11. Lift the hood, the rings and transfer the sandwich to a plate.

12. Repeat the same steps with the remaining ingredients.

★ Serving Suggestion:Serve the sandwich with crispy zucchini fries on the side.
★ Variation Tip:Add a layer of pickled veggies for a change of taste.

NUTRITION FACTS:

Calories 305 | Fat 25g | Sodium 532mg | Carbs 2.3g | Fiber 0.4g | Sugar 2g | Protein 18.3g

RELISHING SALMON AND BACON SANDWIC

PREPARATION TIME: 5 MINUTES | COOKING TIME: 3 MINUTES | SERVINGS: 1

INGREDIENTS

- 2 ounces canned Salmon
- 1 Bacon Slice, cooked
- 2 Bread Slices
- 1 ounce shredded Mozzarella Cheese
- 1 tsp Pickle Relish

- ½ Pickle, sliced
- 1 tsp Dijon Mustard
- 1 tsp Tomato Puree

PREPARATION:

1. Preheat the sandwich maker and grease it with some cooking spray.
2. Cut the bread slices so they can fit the unit.
3. Brush one of the bread slices with Dijon mustard and place it on top of the bottom ring, with the mustard-side up.
4. Add the salmon and bacon on top and sprinkle with the relish and tomato puree.
5. Arrange the pickle slices over and top with the mozzarella.
6. Lower the top ring and add the second bread slice.
7. Cover the unit and cook for about 3 - 4 minutes.
8. Rotate clockwise to open and transfer to a plate.
9. Serve and enjoy!

★ Serving Suggestion: Serve with a side of fresh vegetable sticks.
★ Variation Tip: Add some sliced avocados for a creamier texture.

NUTRITION FACTS:

Calories 420 | Total Fats 34g | Carbs 25g | Protein 28g | Fiber 3.5g

FISH FINGER SANDWICH

PREPARATION TIME: 5 MINUTES | COOKING TIME: 3 MINUTES | SERVINGS: 1

INGREDIENTS

- 2 Fish Fingers, cooked and chopped
- 1 small Hamburger Bun
- 1 tbsp Cream Cheese

- 1 ounce Cheddar Cheese
- 1 tbsp chopped Red Onion

PREPARATION:

1. Preheat the sandwich maker and grease it with some cooking spray.
2. Cut the bun in half and brush it with the cream cheese.
3. Place one half on top of the the bottom ring, with the cream cheese side up.
4. Add the fish finger pieces on top, sprinkle with the red onion and top with the cheddar.
5. Lower the cooking plate and top ring and add the second half of the bun, with the cream cheese down.
6. Close the unit and cook for about 4 minutes.
7. Open carefully and transfer to a plate.
8. Serve and enjoy!

★ Serving Suggestion: Serve with a side of potato wedges.
★ Variation Tip: Add some sliced tomatoes for an extra touch of freshness.

NUTRITION FACTS:

Calories 350 | Total Fats 20g | Carbs 26g | Protein 22g | Fiber 4g

TILAPIA AND PIMENTO DIJON SANDWICH

PREPARATION TIME: 5 MINUTES | COOKING TIME: 3 MINUTES | SERVINGS: 1

INGREDIENTS

- 2 Bread Slices
- 2 ounces chopped cooked Tilapia Fillet
- 1 slice Pimento Cheese
- 2 tsp Dijon Mustard

- ¼ tsp chopped Parsley

PREPARATION:

1. Preheat the sandwich maker and grease it with some cooking spray.
2. Cut the bread slices so they can fit inside the unit, and brush the Dijon over them.
3. Place one bread slice into the bottom ring, with the mustard-side up.
4. Add the tilapia, sprinkle with parsley, and top with cheese.
5. Lower the ring and add the second bread slice, with the mustard-side down.
6. Close the appliance and cook for 3 to 4 minutes.
7. Open carefully and transfer to a plate.
8. Serve and enjoy!

★ Serving Suggestion:Serve with a side of coleslaw.

★ Variation Tip:Add some sliced cucumbers for a crunch.

 **NUTRITION FACTS:**

Calories 388 | Total Fats 13g | Carbs 35g | Protein 29g | Fiber 6g

SALMON AND PISTACHIO MELT

PREPARATION TIME: 5 MINUTES | COOKING TIME: 3 MINUTES | SERVINGS: 1

INGREDIENTS

- 2 Bread Slices
- 2 ounces chopped cooked Salmon
- 2 tsp chopped Pistachios
- 1 ounce shredded Mozzarella

PREPARATION:

1. Preheat and grease the sandwich maker with cooking spray.
2. Cut the bread slices into circles so they can fit perfectly inside the unit.
3. Add the first slice to the bottom ring and place the salmon on top.
4. Add the pistachios over and top with the mozzarella.
5. Lower the top ring and add the remaining bread slice.
6. Close and cook for 3 – 4 minutes.
7. Rotate clockwise and lift open.
8. Transfer to a plate and enjoy!
9. Serve and enjoy!

★ Serving Suggestion:Serve with a side of fresh fruit salad.

★ Variation Tip:Add some sliced onions for an extra flavor boost.

 **NUTRITION FACTS:**

Calories 423 | Total Fats 16g | Carbs 41g | Protein 30.8g | Fiber 7g

COD AND SLAW SANDWICHES WITH TARTAR SAUCE

PREPARATION TIME: 15 MINUTES | COOKING TIME: 15 MINUTES | SERVINGS: 4

INGREDIENTS

- 1 small head cabbage, shredded
- ½ small red onion, sliced
- Salt and black pepper, to taste
- 2 teaspoons cider vinegar

- 1 teaspoon Dijon mustard
- 3 tablespoons mayonnaise
- 1 tablespoon sugar
- Tartar sauce
- 3 tablespoons mayonnaise
- 2 teaspoons sweet pickle relish
- 1 tablespoon capers, rinsed, drained, and chopped
- 1 teaspoon sugar
- 1 teaspoon Dijon mustard

ish

- 2 quarts peanut oil
- 1 ½ cups all-purpose flour
- ½ cup cornstarch
- Salt and black pepper, to taste
- 1 teaspoon baking powder
- ¼ teaspoon paprika
- 12 ounces cod filet, cut into four portions
- 1 cup light beer
- 4 burger buns, split in half

PREPARATION:

1. Mix all the slaw ingredients in a suitable bowl and keep it aside.

2. Whisk all the tartar sauce ingredients in another bowl and set it aside.

3. Mix flour with cornstarch, baking powder, black pepper, salt, paprika and beer in a bowl.

4. Set a deep frying pan with oil over medium-high heat.

5. Dip the fish in the beer batter, then deep fry until golden brown.

6. Transfer the fried fish to a plate lined with parchment paper.

7. Preheat your Hamilton Beach Breakfast Sandwich Maker until PREHEAT light gets green.

8. Lift the top cover, ring, and cooking plate.

9. Place half of a bun, cut-side up, inside the bottom tray of the sandwich maker.

10. Spread ¼ of the fish, slaw and tartar sauce on top.

11. Now lower the cooking plate and top rings.

12. Place the other top half of the bun on top.

13. Cover the top hood, and let the sandwich cook for 5 minutes.

14. Rotate the handle of the cooking plate clockwise until it stops.

15. Lift the hood, the rings and transfer the sandwich to a plate.

16. Repeat the same with the remaining ingredients.

★ Serving Suggestion:Serve the sandwich with a cauliflower bacon salad on the side.
★ Variation Tip:Enjoy sautéed veggies on the side for a change of taste.

 **NUTRITION FACTS:**

Calories 391 | Fat 5g | Sodium 88mg | Carbs 3g | Fiber 0g | Sugar 0g | Protein 27g

MEXICAN-STYLE SEAFOOD BURGER

| PREPARATION TIME: 15 MINUTES | COOKING TIME: 15 MINUTES | SERVINGS: 4 |

INGREDIENTS

- 4 salmon patties
- 1 crunch chopped salad kit
- 4 English muffins, split in half
- 8 ounces hill country fare chipotle mayo

PREPARATION:

1. Sear the salmon patties in a skillet for 5 minutes per side.

2. Preheat your Hamilton Beach Breakfast Sandwich Maker until PREHEAT light gets green.

3. Lift the top cover, ring, and cooking plate.

4. Place half of a muffin, cut-side up, inside the bottom tray of the sandwich maker.

5. Spread ¼ mayonnaise, a salmon patty and ¼ chopped salad on top.

6. Now lower the cooking plate and top rings.

7. Place the other top half of the muffin on top.

8. Cover the top hood, and let the burger cook for 5 minutes.

9. Rotate the handle of the cooking plate clockwise until it stops.

10. Lift the hood, the rings and transfer the burger to a plate.

11. Repeat the same steps with the remaining ingredients.

★ Serving Suggestion:Serve the sandwich with a cauliflower bacon salad on the side.
★ Variation Tip:Add a layer of sliced bell peppers for a change of taste.

NUTRITION FACTS:

Calories 361 | Fat 16g | Sodium 515mg | Carbs 29.3g | Fiber 0.1g | Sugar 18.2g | Protein 33.3g

MAYO SHRIMP SANDWICH

| PREPARATION TIME: 15 MINUTES | COOKING TIME: 5 MINUTES | SERVINGS: 4 |

INGREDIENTS

- 1 cup shrimp, peeled, deveined, cooked and chopped
- 4 tablespoons mayonnaise
- 1 teaspoon lemon juice
- 1 teaspoon dried dill
- 4 burger buns

PREPARATION:

1. Combine all ingredients except buns.

2. Preheat your Hamilton Beach Breakfast Sandwich Maker.

3. Lift the top cover, ring, and cooking plate.

4. Place the lower half of the bun in the sandwich maker and top it with ¼th of the shrimp mixture.

5. Now lower the cooking plate and top rings.

6. Place the other top half of the bun on top.

7. Cover the top hood, and let the sandwich cook for 5 minutes.

8. When finished cooking, rotate the handle of the cooking plate clockwise until it stops.

9. Lift the hood, the rings and transfer the sandwich to a plate.

10. Repeat the same steps with remaining ingredients.

★ Serving Suggestion:Serve the sandwich with your favorite sauce on the side.
★ Variation Tip:Add some additional dried herbs to the filling.

NUTRITION FACTS:

Calories 330| Fat 10.4 g | Sodium 690 mg | Carbs 11.4 g | Fiber 3 g | Sugar 4.7g | Protein 48 g

LOBSTER ROLLS WITH BASIL

| PREPARATION TIME: 15 MINUTES | COOKING TIME: 5 MINUTES | SERVINGS: 4 |

INGREDIENTS

- 1 tablespoon butter, softened
- 4 English muffins, split
- 4 large leaf (blank)s lettuce leaves
- 1½ lbs. cooked and cubed lobster meat
- 2 tablespoons mayonnaise
- 1 teaspoon fresh lime juice

- 1 dash hot pepper sauce
- 2 medium green onions, chopped
- 1 stalk celery, chopped
- 1 pinch salt and black pepper to taste
- 1 pinch dried basil

PREPARATION:

1. Mix lobster meat with butter, mayonnaise, lime juice, hot pepper sauce, green onion, black pepper, salt, basil and celery in a bowl.

2. Preheat your Hamilton Beach Breakfast Sandwich Maker until PREHEAT light gets green.

3. Lift the top cover, ring, and cooking plate.

4. Place half of the English muffin, cut-side up, inside the bottom tray of the sandwich maker.

5. Arrange a lettuce leaf on top of the English muffin, then add ¼ of the lobster mixture on top.

6. Now lower the cooking plate and top rings.

7. Place the other top half of the muffin on top.

8. Cover the top hood, and let the sandwich cook for 5 minutes.

9. Rotate the handle of the cooking plate clockwise until it stops.

10. Lift the hood, the rings and transfer the sandwich to a plate.

11. Repeat the same steps with the remaining ingredients.

★ Serving Suggestion:Serve the sandwich with crispy carrot chips on the side.
★ Variation Tip:Add a layer of pickled onions for a change of taste.

NUTRITION FACTS:

Calories 380 | Fat 20g | Sodium 686mg | Carbs 3g | Fiber 1g | Sugar 1.2g | Protein 21g

MAYO SCALLOP CORN BURGERS

PREPARATION TIME: 15 MINUTES

COOKING TIME: 5 MINUTES

SERVINGS: 6

INGREDIENTS

- ½ cup mayonnaise
- 3 tablespoons ketchup
- 1 teaspoon Tabasco sauce
- Salt and black pepper, to taste
- 3 ears of corn, shucked
- 1½ lbs. sea scallops, chopped
- 6 soft hamburger buns, split
- 6 lettuce leaves
- 6 thick tomato slices
- 12 slices cooked thick-cut bacon

PREPARATION:

1. Mix scallops with corn, black pepper, tabasco sauce, ketchup and mayonnaise in a bowl.

2. Preheat your Hamilton Beach Breakfast Sandwich Maker until PREHEAT light gets green.

3. Lift the top cover, ring, and cooking plate.

4. Place half of a bun, cut-side up, inside the bottom tray of the sandwich maker.

5. Arrange a lettuce leaf on top then add ⅙ of the scallop mixture, 1 lettuce leaf, a tomato slice and 2 bacon slices on top.

6. Now lower the cooking plate and top rings.

7. Place the other top half of the bun on top.

8. Cover the top hood, and let the sandwich cook for 5 minutes.

9. Rotate the handle of the cooking plate clockwise until it stops.

10. Lift the hood, the rings and transfer the sandwich to a plate.

11. Repeat the same steps with the remaining ingredients.

★ Serving Suggestion:Serve the sandwich with crispy fries on the side.
★ Variation Tip:Add a layer of pickled veggies for a change of taste.

NUTRITION FACTS:

Calories 282 | Fat 15g | Sodium 526mg | Carbs 20g | Fiber 0.6g | Sugar 3.3g | Protein 16g

LEMONY SHRIMP COD BURGERS

PREPARATION TIME: 15 MINUTES | **COOKING TIME: 15 MINUTES** | **SERVINGS: 4**

INGREDIENTS

- 12 ounces medium shrimp, peeled, deveined, and cut into chunks
- 8 ounces cod, cut into chunks
- ¾ cup fresh breadcrumbs
- ¼ cup drained capers, rinsed
- 2 medium scallions, sliced
- 3 tablespoons chopped parsley
- ¼ cup lemon juice
- 1 ¼ teaspoon salt
- 3/4 teaspoon black pepper
- Vegetable oil, for brushing
- 4 hamburger buns, split in half

PREPARATION:

1. Blend shrimp, cod, crumbs, capers, scallions, parsley, lemon juice, black pepper and salt in a food processor for 1 minute.

2. Make 4 patties out of this mixture and sear them in a skillet greased with oil for 5 minutes per side.

3. Preheat your Hamilton Beach Breakfast Sandwich Maker until PREHEAT light gets green.

4. Lift the top cover, ring, and cooking plate.

5. Place half of a bun, cut-side up, inside the bottom tray of the sandwich maker.

6. Now lower the cooking plate and top rings.

7. Place a patty, a lettuce leaf and the other top half of the bun on top.

8. Cover the top hood, and let the burger cook for 5 minutes.

9. Rotate the handle of the cooking plate clockwise until it stops.

10. Lift the hood, the rings and transfer the burger to a plate.

11. Repeat the same steps with the remaining ingredients.

★ Serving Suggestion:Serve the sandwich with crispy fries on the side.
★ Variation Tip:Add a layer of spicy mayo and pickled veggies for a change of taste.

NUTRITION FACTS:

Calories 325 | Fat 16g | Sodium 431mg | Carbs 2g | Fiber 1.2g | Sugar 4g | Protein 23g

MAYO SHRIMP SALAD BURGERS

PREPARATION TIME: 15 MINUTES | **COOKING TIME: 5 MINUTES** | **SERVINGS: 2**

INGREDIENTS

- 1 cup shrimp, peeled, deveined, cooked and chopped
- 4 tablespoons mayonnaise
- 1 teaspoon lemon juice
- 1 tablespoon green onion, chopped
- 1 teaspoon Old Bay seasoning
- 2 burger buns, split

PREPARATION:

1. In a bowl, combine all the ingredients except burger buns.

2. Preheat your Hamilton Beach Breakfast Sandwich Maker.

3. Lift the top cover, ring, and cooking plate.

4. Add burger bun bottoms inside and top with ½ of the mayo mixture.

5. Spread with ½ of the shrimp mixture.

6. Now lower the cooking plate and top rings.

7. Add the other bun half on top.

8. Cover the top hood, and let the sandwich cook for 5 minutes.

9. When finished cooking, rotate the handle of the cooking plate clockwise until it stops.

10. Lift the hood, the rings and transfer the sandwich to a plate.

11. Repeat the same steps with remaining ingredients.

★ Serving Suggestion:Serve the sandwich with crispy bacon and your favorite sauce on the side.

★ Variation Tip:You can add a lettuce leave to the filling as well.

 **NUTRITION FACTS:**

Calories 352 | Fat 9.1g | Sodium 1294mg | Carbs 3.9g | Fiber 1g | Sugar 1g | Protein 61g

FRUIT SALAD SANDWICH WITH LEMON

 PREPARATION TIME: 10 MINUTES

 COOKING TIME: 6 MINUTES

 SERVINGS: 1

INGREDIENTS

- 1 store bought or homemade biscuit
- 1 Tbsp. strawberry flavored cream cheese
- A few slices of banana, apple, grapes, peaches, or any fruit of choice
- 1 tsp. fresh lemon juice
- Chopped mint leaves

PREPARATION:

1. Preheat the breakfast sandwich maker.

2. Cut the biscuit in half.

3. Spread strawberry flavored cream cheese on the inside of both biscuit halves.

4. Arrange the fruit slices on one half of the biscuit.

5. Sprinkle fresh lemon juice and chopped mint leaves over the fruit.

6. Place the other biscuit half on top.

7. Put the sandwich in the sandwich maker and cook for 6 minutes.

8. Carefully remove and enjoy!

★ **Serving Suggestion:** For the Fruit Salad Sandwich With Lemon, serve with a side of yogurt.

★ **Variation Tip:** For the Fruit Salad Sandwich With Lemon, you can add a dollop of whipped cream.

 **NUTRITION FACTS:**

Calories: 300 | Fat: 10g | Carbs: 45g | Protein: 5g | Fiber: 5g

CINNAMON RAISIN APPLE SANDWICH

 PREPARATION TIME: 5 MINUTES

 COOKING TIME: 5 MINUTES

 SERVINGS: 1

INGREDIENTS

- 2 slices cinnamon raisin bread
- ½ small apple, sliced thin
- 1 thin slice cheddar cheese
- ½ teaspoon unsalted butter
- Pinch ground cinnamon and nutmeg

PREPARATION:

1. Preheat the breakfast sandwich maker.

2. Place one slice of bread inside the bottom tray of the sandwich maker. Spread the bread with butter.

3. Top the bread with the slices of apple then sprinkle them with cinnamon and nutmeg.

4. Place the slice of cheddar cheese over the apples.

5. Top the cheese with the other piece of bread.

6. Close the sandwich maker and cook for 4 to 5 minutes until it is heated through.

7. Carefully open the sandwich maker and enjoy your sandwich!

 **NUTRITION FACTS:**

Calories: 280 | Fat: 12g | Carbs: 35g | Protein: 8g | Fiber: 3g

 **NUTRITION FACTS:**

Calories: 450 | Fat: 25g | Carbs: 55g | Protein: 5g | Fiber: 3g

CARAMEL STRAWBERRIES SANDWICH

HONEY BLUEBERRY AND PEAR CROISSANT

PREPARATION TIME: 15 MINUTES | COOKING TIME: 5 MINUTES | SERVINGS: 2

INGREDIENTS

- 2 medium croissants, sliced in half
- 1 large pear (bosc pears are a perfect choice), sliced
- 2 tablespoons of honey
- ½ cup of blueberries, rinsed, drained and dried
- 3 tablespoons of cream cheese, brought to room temperature

PREPARATION:

1. Preheat your Hamilton Beach Breakfast Sandwich Maker.

2. Lift the top cover, ring, and cooking plate.

3. Take 1 ½ teaspoons of the cream cheese, spreading half of it on the top of the croissant and half on the croissant bottom.

4. Place the croissant bottom in the bottom slot of the sandwich maker, topped with half of the pear slices.

5. Add ¼ cup of blueberries on top of the pear slices.

6. Take a tablespoon of the honey, drizzling it

PREPARATION TIME: 5 MINUTES | COOKING TIME: 5 MINUTES | SERVINGS: 4

INGREDIENTS

- 4 Butter Croissants, large
- 4 tbsp. Caramel Sauce, salted
- 8 sliced Strawberries
- 9 Marshmallows, large, cut into slices
- Cooking spray

PREPARATION:

1. Slice the croissants in half. Spread ½ tbsp. of caramel on each.

2. On one of the sides layer the strawberry slices and on the other layer the marshmallow slices.

3. Bring the sides together to make a sandwich.

4. Preheat the sandwich maker and spray with a cooking spray

5. Cook the sandwiches for 2 minutes and flip. Cook for 2 more minutes

6. Remove and let it rest for 1 minute

7. Cut in half and serve.

carefully over the fruit.

7. Now lower the cooking plate and top rings, then place the other top half of croissant on top.

8. Cover the top hood, and let the sandwich cook for 5 minutes.

9. When finished cooking, rotate the handle of the cooking plate clockwise until it stops.

10. Lift the hood, the rings and transfer the sandwich to a plate.

11. Repeat the same steps with remaining ingredients.

★ Serving Suggestion:Serve the sandwich with crispy bacon and your favorite sauce on the side.

★ Variation Tip:You can add a lettuce leave to the filling as well.

NUTRITION FACTS:

Calories 245 | Fat 14g | Sodium 122mg | Carbs 23.3g | Fiber 1.2g | Sugar 12g | Protein 4.3g

APPLE SANDWICH WITH STRAWBERRY JAM

PREPARATION TIME: 15 MINUTES | COOKING TIME: 5 MINUTES | SERVINGS: 2

INGREDIENTS

- 4 slices whole-wheat bread, cut in 4-inch circle
- ½ teaspoons light butter
- ½ apple, sliced
- 1 tablespoon strawberry jam

PREPARATION:

1. Preheat your Hamilton Beach Breakfast Sandwich Maker.

2. Lift the top cover, ring, and cooking plate.

3. Place a bread round in the sandwich maker.

4. Spread ½ of the butter and jam on top.

---

5. Now lower the cooking plate and top rings, then place ½ of the apple, and other bread slice or top.

6. Cover the top hood, and let the sandwich cook for 5 minutes.

7. When finished cooking, rotate the handle of the cooking plate clockwise until it stops.

8. Lift the hood, the rings and transfer the sandwich to a plate.

9. Repeat the same steps with remaining ingredients.

★ Serving Suggestion:Serve the sandwich with your favorite sauce on the side.

★ Variation Tip:You can add a drizzle of lemon juice on top of the filling as well.

NUTRITION FACTS:

Calories 198 | Fat 14g | Sodium 272mg | Carbs 34g | Fiber 1g | Sugar 9.3g | Protein 1.3g

HONEY NUT MIX SANDWICH

PREPARATION TIME: 15 MINUTES | COOKING TIME: 5 MINUTES | SERVINGS: 2

INGREDIENTS

- 4 slices whole-wheat bread, cut in 4-inch circle
- ½ teaspoons light butter
- ¼ cup roasted mixed nuts (almonds, pecans, walnuts, cashews, etc.)
- 1 tablespoon wild honey

PREPARATION:

1. Mix together the mixed nuts and honey.

2. Make two sandwiches with the honeyed mixed nuts.

3. Preheat your Hamilton Beach Breakfast Sandwich Maker.

4. Lift the top cover, ring, and cooking plate. Lightly pat butter on each sandwich maker pan.

5. Place one sandwich in the sandwich maker.

6. Now lower the cooking plate and top.

7. Cover the top hood, and let the sandwich cook for 5 minutes.

8. When finished cooking, rotate the handle of the cooking plate clockwise until it stops.

9. Lift the hood, the rings and transfer the sandwich to a plate.

10. Repeat the same steps with remaining ingredients.

★ Serving Suggestion:Serve the sandwich with coleslaw and your favorite sauce on the side.
★ Variation Tip:You can add a drizzle of paprika on top of the filling as well.

 **NUTRITION FACTS:**

Calories 173 | Fat 9.8g | Sodium 112.2mg | Carbs 17.5g | Fiber 1.2g | Sugar 12.2g | Protein 3.9g

SWEET MANGO-PEACH SANDWICH

 PREPARATION TIME: 15 MINUTES | COOKING TIME: 5 MINUTES | SERVINGS: 2

INGREDIENTS

- 4 slices whole-wheat bread, cut in 4-inch circle
- ½ teaspoons light butter
- ½ mango, sliced
- 1 peach, sliced
- 2 teaspoons pure maple syrup or wild honey

PREPARATION:

1. Spread the honey or maple syrup on each bread slice.

2. Make two sandwiches, layering mango and peach slices.

3. Preheat your Hamilton Beach Breakfast Sandwich Maker.

4. Lift the top cover, ring, and cooking plate.

5. Lightly pat butter on each sandwich maker pan. Place a sandwich in the sandwich maker.

6. Now lower the cooking plate and top rings.

7. Cover the top hood, and let the sandwich cook for 5 minutes.

8. When finished cooking, rotate the handle of the cooking plate clockwise until it stops.

9. Lift the hood, the rings and transfer the sandwich to a plate.

10. Repeat the same steps with remaining ingredients.

★ Serving Suggestion:Serve the sandwich with your favorite sauce on the side.
★ Variation Tip:Add some additional ground black pepper to the filling.

 **NUTRITION FACTS:**

Calories 297 | Fat 2.1g | Sodium 248.1mg | Carbs 64.9g | Fiber 3.9g | Sugar 9g | Protein 5.5g

CHEDDAR-APPLE SMOKED BACON SANDWICH

 PREPARATION TIME: 5 MINUTES | COOKING TIME: 4 MINUTES | SERVINGS: 1

INGREDIENTS

- 1 English muffin, split
- 1 tsp. grainy mustard
- 2 slices smoked bacon
- 3 thin apple slices
- 1 slice cheddar cheese
- 1 egg

PREPARATION:

1. Spread the mustard on one half of the English muffin. Place muffin, mustard side up, into the bottom ring of breakfast sandwich maker. Place smoked bacon, apple slices and cheddar cheese on top.

2. Lower the cooking plate and top ring; crack an egg into the egg plate and pierce to break the yolk; top with other English muffin half.

3. Close the cover and cook for 4 to 5 minutes or until egg is cooked through. Gently slide the egg plate out and remove sandwich with a rubber spatula.

★ Serving Suggestion:Serve with a side of fresh fruit or a small salad.
★ Variation Tip:You could add some spinach leaves for an extra boost of nutrients.

 **NUTRITION FACTS:**

Calories: 450 | Fat: 25g | Carbs: 35g | Protein: 20g | Fiber: 3g

GRUYERE, APPLE AND HAM SANDWICH

PREPARATION TIME: 3 MINUTES | **COOKING TIME: 5 MINUTES** | **SERVINGS: 1**

INGREDIENTS

- 1 Ciabatta roll, sliced in half
- 1 slice ham
- A few apple slices
- 1 slice gruyere cheese
- 1 Tbsp. milk
- 2 tsp. diced onion
- 1 egg
- Sea salt and pepper

PREPARATION:

1. Place one Ciabatta roll half into the bottom ring of breakfast sandwich maker. Place ham, apple slices and gruyere cheese on top.

2. In a small bowl whisk together milk, onion, egg, sea salt and pepper. Lower the cooking plate and top ring; pour egg mixture into egg plate. Top with other roll half.

3. Close the cover and cook for 4 to 5 minutes or until egg is cooked and cheese is melted. Remove sandwich with a rubber spatula.

★ Serving Suggestion:Serve with a side of potato chips or a small green salad.
★ Variation Tip:Replace the ham with turkey or add some sliced cucumber for extra crunch.

 **NUTRITION FACTS:**

Calories: 450| Fat: 25g |Carbs: 35g |Protein: 20g |Fiber: 3g |Sodium: 700mg

BLUEBERRY WAFFLE SANDWICH

 **PREPARATION TIME: 5 MINUTES** **COOKING TIME: 5 MINUTES** **SERVINGS: 1**

INGREDIENTS

- 2 small store bought frozen blueberry waffles
- Butter
- 2 strips bacon
- 1 slice cheddar cheese
- 1 egg

- Sea salt and pepper

PREPARATION:

1. Spread butter on both waffles. Place one into the bottom ring of breakfast sandwich maker, butter side down. Place bacon and cheddar cheese on top.

2. Lower the cooking plate and top ring; crack an egg into the egg plate and pierce to break the yolk. Season with sea salt and pepper. Top with the other waffle.

3. Close the cover and cook for 4 to 5 minutes or until the egg is cooked and the cheese is melted. Remove the sandwich with a rubber spatula.

★ Serving Suggestion:Serve with a side of maple syrup or fresh fruit.
★ Variation Tip:Add some sliced avocado or a spoonful of salsa for an extra flavor boost.

 **NUTRITION FACTS:**

Calories: 550 Fat: 30g |Carbs: 45g| Protein: 20g| Fiber: 3g |Sodium: 800mg

APPLE AND BRIE CROISSANT SANDWICH

PREPARATION TIME: 5 MINUTES | COOKING TIME: 4 MINUTES | SERVINGS: 1

INGREDIENTS

- 2 Apple Slices
- 1 ounce Brie, crumbled
- 1 Croissant
- 2 tsp Cream Cheese

PREPARATION:

1. Preheat and grease the sandwich maker.

2. Cut the croissant in half and spread one teaspoon of cream cheese over each half.

3. When the green light appears, place one of the croissant halves into the bottom ring, with the cut-side up.

4. Top with the apple slices and brie.

5. Lower the top ring and cooking plate and place the other croissant half inside.

6. Close and cook for 4 minutes.

7. Turn the handle clockwise, open, and transfer to a plate.

8. Serve and enjoy!

★ Serving Suggestion:For the Apple And Brie Croissant Sandwich, enjoy with a glass of apple cider.
★ Variation Tip:For the Apple And Brie Croissant Sandwich, sprinkle some chopped nuts on top for added crunch.

 **NUTRITION FACTS:**

Calories 369 | Total Fats 23g | Carbs 29g | Protein 11g | Fiber 2g

PINEAPPLE AND COCONUT FILLED CROISSANT SANDWICH

PREPARATION TIME: 5 MINUTES | COOKING TIME: 4 MINUTES | SERVINGS: 1

INGREDIENTS

- 1 small croissant, sliced in half
- 1 Tbsp. cream cheese
- 1 – 2 Tbsp. finely chopped pineapple
- Shredded coconut
- Honey

PREPARATION:

1. Spread cream cheese on both croissant halves. Place one half into the bottom ring of

breakfast sandwich maker, cut side up. Place chopped pineapple and shredded coconut on top. Drizzle with honey.

2. Lower the cooking plate and top ring; top with other croissant half.

3. Close the cover and cook for 3 to 4 minutes or until sandwich is warmed through.

4. Open sandwich maker and remove sandwich.

★ Serving Suggestion:Serve with a cup of freshly brewed coffee or tea.
★ Variation Tip:You can also add a few slices of fresh banana for added sweetness.

 NUTRITION FACTS:

Calories: 350 |Total Fat: 18g |Saturated Fat: 10g |Trans Fat: 0g| Cholesterol: 35mg |Sodium: 200mg| Total Carbohydrate: 42g |Dietary Fiber: 2g |Sugars: 18g |Protein: 6g

BERRY PANCAKE

PREPARATION TIME: 5 MINUTES | COOKING TIME: 4 MINUTES | SERVINGS: 1

INGREDIENTS

- 1 Frozen Pancake
- ¼ cup chopped frozen Berries
- 1 tsp Sugar
- 1 tbsp Whipped Cream

PREPARATION:

1. Preheat the sandwich maker and grease it with some cooking spray.

2. Place the pancake on top of the bottom ring.

3. Arrange the berries over and sprinkle with the sugar.

4. Close the lid and cook for 3 – 4 minutes.

5. Open carefully and transfer to a plate.

6. Top with the whipped Cream and enjoy!

★ Serving Suggestion:Serve with a side of maple syrup for added sweetness.

★ Variation Tip:Replace the frozen berries with fresh berries for a more intense flavor.

 NUTRITION FACTS:

Calories 117 |Total Fats 2g |Carbs 23g |Protein 2.3g |Fiber 2g |Sodium 125mg

SPICY CREAM CHEESE RASPBERRY CROISSANT

PREPARATION TIME: 5 MINUTES | COOKING TIME: 3 MINUTES | SERVINGS: 1

INGREDIENTS

- 1 small croissant, sliced in half
- 1 – 2 Tbsp. cream cheese
- 1 – 2 Tbsp. raspberry jam
- 1 small jalapeño, seeded and sliced in thin rings

PREPARATION:

1. Spread cream cheese and raspberry jam on bottom half of croissant. Place in the bottom of breakfast sandwich maker. Sprinkle with a few jalapeño rings (to taste).

2. Lower cooking plate and top ring. Place other half of croissant on top and close the sandwich maker lid. Cook for 2 – 3 minutes or until the cream cheese is melted and sandwich is warm. Carefully remove from sandwich maker and enjoy!

★ Serving Suggestion:Serve with a glass of cold milk for a balanced treat.
★ Variation Tip:Replace the raspberry jam with strawberry jam for a different flavor.

NUTRITION FACTS:

Calories: 320| Total Fat: 15g |Saturated Fat: 8g |Trans Fat: 0g| Cholesterol: 30mg| Sodium: 180mg| Total Carbohydrate: 40g| Dietary Fiber: 2g |Sugars: 15g| Protein: 5g

MAPLE APPLE SANDWICH

 PREPARATION TIME: 15 MINUTES
 COOKING TIME: 5 MINUTES
 SERVINGS: 2

INGREDIENTS

- 4 slices whole-wheat bread, cut in 4-inch circle
- ½ teaspoons light butter
- ½ apple, sliced
- 1 teaspoon ground cinnamon
- 2 teaspoons pure maple syrup

PREPARATION:

1. Spread maple syrup on each bread slice.

2. Make two sandwiches, layering apple slices, and sprinkles of cinnamon powder.

3. Preheat your Hamilton Beach Breakfast Sandwich Maker.

4. Lift the top cover, ring, and cooking plate. Lightly pat butter on each sandwich maker pan.

5. Place a sandwich in the sandwich maker.

6. Now lower the cooking plate and top rings.

7. Cover the top hood, and let the sandwich cook for 5 minutes.

8. When finished cooking, rotate the handle of the cooking plate clockwise until it stops.

9. Lift the hood, the rings and transfer the sandwich to a plate.

10. Repeat the same steps with remaining ingredients.

★ Serving Suggestion:Serve the sandwich with crispy bacon and your favorite sauce on the side.

★ Variation Tip:Add some additional dried herbs to the filling.

 **NUTRITION FACTS:**

Calories 266 | Fat 11.8g | Sodium 267mg | Carbs 37.6g | Fiber 2.3g | Sugar 5g | Protein 2.2g | Calcium 30mg |

PEANUT BUTTER BANANA SANDWICH

 PREPARATION TIME: 15 MINUTES — COOKING TIME: 5 MINUTES — SERVINGS: 2

INGREDIENTS

- 4 slices whole-wheat bread, cut in 4-inch circle
- ½ teaspoons light butter
- 1 medium banana, slightly crushed
- 1 tablespoon peanut butter

PREPARATION:

1. Make two sandwiches, layering peanut butter spread and crushed bananas.

2. Preheat your Hamilton Beach Breakfast Sandwich Maker.

3. Lift the top cover, ring, and cooking plate.

4. Lightly pat butter on each sandwich maker pan.

5. Place a sandwich in the sandwich maker.

6. Now lower the cooking plate and top rings.

7. Cover the top hood, and let the sandwich cook for 5 minutes.

8. When finished cooking, rotate the handle of the cooking plate clockwise until it stops.

9. Lift the hood, the rings and transfer the sandwich to a plate.

10. Repeat the same steps with remaining ingredients.

NUTRITION FACTS:

Calories 121 | Fat 7.1g | Sodium 110mg | Carbs 5g | Fiber 0.5g | Sugar 1.1g | Protein 10g | Potassium 150mg | Magnesium 10mg

DARK CHOCOLATE SANDWICH WITH CHERRIES

 PREPARATION TIME: 15 MINUTES

 COOKING TIME: 5 MINUTES

 SERVINGS: 2

INGREDIENTS

- 4 slices whole-wheat bread, cut in 4-inch circle
- ½ teaspoons light butter
- ¼ cup cherries, slightly crushed
- 6 squares dark chocolate 70% cocoa, slightly crushed

PREPARATION:

1. Mix together the cherries and dark chocolate.
2. Make two sandwiches with the chocolate and cherry mixture.
3. Preheat your Hamilton Beach Breakfast Sandwich Maker.
4. Lift the top cover, ring, and cooking plate.
5. Lightly pat butter on each sandwich maker pan.
6. Place a sandwich in the sandwich maker.
7. Now lower the cooking plate and top rings.
8. Cover the top hood, and let the sandwich cook for 5 minutes.

9. When finished cooking, rotate the handle of the cooking plate clockwise until it stops.
10. Lift the hood, the rings and transfer the sandwich to a plate.
11. Repeat the same steps with remaining ingredients.

NUTRITION FACTS:

Calories 186 | Fat 9g | Sodium 124mg | Carbs 23g | Fiber 0.4g | Sugar 11.5g | Protein 3.2g | Iron 0.8mg | Phosphorus 50mg

PEACH BRAN SANDWICH

PREPARATION TIME: 15 MINUTES

COOKING TIME: 5 MINUTES

SERVINGS: 2

INGREDIENTS

- 4 bran bread slices, cut into 4 inches round
- 2 tablespoon peach preserves
- 1 peach, peeled and sliced

PREPARATION:

1. Preheat your Hamilton Beach Breakfast Sandwich Maker until PREHEAT light gets green.
2. Lift the top cover, ring, and cooking plate.
3. Place a bread slice, inside the bottom tray of the sandwich maker.
4. Spread ½ of the preserves, and peach slices on top.
5. Now lower the cooking plate and top rings then.
6. Place the other bread slice on top.

7. Cover the top hood, and let the sandwich cook for 5 minutes.

8. Rotate the handle of the cooking plate clockwise until it stops.

9. Lift the hood, the rings and transfer the sandwich to a plate.

10. Repeat the same steps with the remaining ingredients.

★ Serving Suggestion:Serve the sandwich with a glass of orange juice on the side.
★ Variation Tip:You can add a drizzle of chocolate chips to the filling as well.

NUTRITION FACTS:

Calories 282 | Fat 15g | Sodium 526mg | Carbs 20g | Fiber 0.6g | Sugar 3.3g | Protein 16g | Vitamin C 5mg | Zinc 0.5mg

APPLE, PINEAPPLE, AND BANANA SANDWICH

PREPARATION TIME: 15 MINUTES | COOKING TIME: 5 MINUTES | SERVINGS: 2

INGREDIENTS

- 4 whole wheat brown bread, cut into 4 inches round
- 2 ripe bananas, peeled and sliced
- 2 pineapples, sliced thin
- 1 apple, sliced
- 2 tablespoon mixed fruit jam

PREPARATION:

1. Preheat your Hamilton Beach Breakfast Sandwich Maker until PREHEAT light gets green.

2. Lift the top cover, ring, and cooking plate.

3. Place a bread slice, inside the bottom tray of the sandwich maker.

4. Spread ½ of the jam, apple, pineapple and

---

bananas.

5. Place the other bread slice on top.

6. Now lower the cooking plate and top rings then.

7. Cover the top hood, and let the sandwich cook for 5 minutes.

8. Rotate the handle of the cooking plate clockwise until it stops.

9. Lift the hood, the rings and transfer the sandwich to a plate.

10. Repeat the same steps with the remaining ingredients.

★ Serving Suggestion:Serve the sandwich with an avocado smoothie on the side.
★ Variation Tip:You can add a drizzle of sprinkles to the filling as well.

NUTRITION FACTS:

Calories 282 | Fat 15g | Sodium 526mg | Carbs 20g | Fiber 0.6g | Sugar 3.3g | Protein 16g | Vitamin B6 0.2mg | Copper 0.1mg

JAPANESE FRUIT SANDWICH WITH STRAWBERRIES, KIWIS, AND ORANGES

PREPARATION TIME: 15 MINUTES | COOKING TIME: 5 MINUTES | SERVINGS: 2

INGREDIENTS

- 12 strawberries, sliced
- 2 kiwis, sliced
- 1 navel orange, sliced

- 4 slices shokupan (Japanese Pullman loaf bread), cut into 4-inch rounds
- Whipped cream
- 1 cup heavy whipping cream
- 5 teaspoons sugar
- 1 teaspoon rum

PREPARATION:

1. Mix the heavy whipping cream with rum and sugar in a bowl until whipped.

2. Preheat your Hamilton Beach Breakfast Sandwich Maker until the PREHEAT light turns green.

3. Lift the top cover, ring, and cooking plate.

4. Place a bread slice in the bottom tray of the sandwich maker.

5. Add half of the whipped cream, followed by slices of orange, kiwi, and strawberry.

6. Place another bread slice on top.

7. Lower the cooking plate and top rings.

8. Cover the top hood and let the sandwich cook for 5 minutes.

9. Rotate the handle of the cooking plate clockwise until it stops.

10. Lift the hood, the rings, and transfer the sandwich to a plate.

11. Repeat the same steps with the remaining ingredients.

★ Serving Suggestion: Serve the sandwich along with an apple smoothie.

★ Variation Tip: You could also add a drizzle of chocolate chips to the filling.

NUTRITION FACTS:

Calories 284 | Fat 16g | Sodium 252mg | Carbs 31.6g | Fiber 0.9g | Sugar 6.6g | Protein 3.7g

EGGPLANT SANDWICH

PREPARATION TIME: 15 MINUTES

COOKING TIME: 20 MINUTES

SERVINGS: 4

INGREDIENTS

For the filling:
- ¾ cup of Mayo
- 1/3 cup Basil, chopped
- 3 tbsp. Parmesan cheese, grated
- 2 tbsp. Chives, minced

For the tortilla cups:
- Flour Tortilla
- 1 ounce shredded Cheddar
- 1 tsp Sour Cream
- 1 tsp Salsa
- 2 ounces cooked Ground Chicken
- 2 tsp chopped Onion
- 1 tsp chopped Parsley

PREPARATION:

1. Preheat and grease the sandwich maker.

2. Slide out the cooking plate – you will not need it for this recipe.

3. Place the tortilla into the ring, tucking it, so that it looks like a cup.

4. In a small bowl, combine the rest of the ingredients for the filling.

5. Fill the taco cup with the chicken filling.

6. Close the lid and cook for 5 minutes.

7. Rotate clockwise and lift to open, then transfer to a plate.

8. Serve and enjoy!

 ★ Serving Suggestion:Serve with a side of guacamole and some fresh cut vegetables.

★ Variation Tip:Replace the ground chicken with ground turkey for a different flavor.

NUTRITION FACTS:

Calories 305 | Total Fats 14.5g |Carbs 19.6g | Protein 23.2g |Fiber 1.3g

TOMATO BASIL FLATBREAD

PREPARATION TIME: 5 MINUTES

COOKING TIME: 5 MINUTES

SERVINGS: 1

INGREDIENTS

- 1 small round flatbread
- 1 tsp. olive oil
- Salt and pepper to taste
- 1 thick slice ripe tomato
- 4 fresh basil leaves
- 1 slice fresh mozzarella cheese
- 1 large egg

PREPARATION:

1. Preheat the breakfast sandwich maker.

2. Place the round flatbread inside the bottom tray of the sandwich maker.

3. Brush the flatbread with the olive oil and sprinkle with salt and pepper.

4. Top the flatbread with the slice of tomato, basil leaves and mozzarella cheese.

5. Slide the egg tray into place and crack the egg into it. Use a fork to stir the egg, just breaking the yolk.

6. Close the sandwich maker and cook for 4 to 5 minutes until the egg is cooked through.

7. Carefully rotate the egg tray out of the sandwich maker then open the sandwich maker to enjoy your sandwich.

★ Serving Suggestion:Serve with a side of fresh fruit salad.

★ Variation Tip:Add some slices of cooked bacon for a savory boost.

 **NUTRITION FACTS:**

Calories: 320 |Total Fat: 18g| Saturated Fat: 6g |Trans Fat: 0g| Cholesterol: 180mg| Sodium: 450mg| Total Carbohydrate: 25g |Dietary Fiber: 2g |Sugars: 3g |Protein: 15g

BEANS & VEGGIES SANDWICH

PREPARATION TIME: 5 MINUTES | **COOKING TIME: 8 MINUTES** | **SERVINGS: 1**

INGREDIENTS

- 2 slices multigrain bread
- 2 Tbsp. canned black beans
- 2 tsp. diced green onion
- 2 tsp. shredded carrot
- 2 tsp. shredded radish
- 1 slice Pepper Jack cheese
- 1 egg
- Sea salt and pepper

PREPARATION:

1. Spread black beans on both slices of bread. Place one slice, beans side up, into the bottom ring of sandwich maker. Sprinkle green onion, carrot and radish on top. Top with Pepper Jack cheese.

2. Lower the cooking plate and top ring; crack an egg into the egg plate and pierce to break the

yolk. Season with sea salt and pepper. Top with other slice of bread.

3. Close the cover and cook for 4 to 5 minutes or until egg is cooked through. Gently slide the egg plate out and remove sandwich with a rubber spatula.

★ Serving Suggestion:Serve with a side of fresh fruit salad or a small bowl of yogurt.

★ Variation Tip:You could add some sliced tomatoes or cucumber for extra crunch and freshness.

 **NUTRITION FACTS:**

Calories 350| Fat: 12|Carbs: 40g |Protein: 18g| Fiber: 8g| Sodium: 450mg

SPINACH HAVARTI SANDWICH

PREPARATION TIME: 5 MINUTES | **COOKING TIME: 4 MINUTES** | **SERVINGS: 1**

INGREDIENTS

- 1 English muffin
- 2 tsp. mayonnaise
- ½ tsp. yellow mustard
- A few baby spinach leaves
- 1 slice Havarti cheese
- 1 egg
- Sea salt and pepper

PREPARATION:

1. Spread the mayonnaise and mustard on both halves of the English muffin. Place one half, mayo/mustard side up into the bottom ring of the breakfast sandwich maker. Place the baby spinach leaves and Havarti cheese on top.

2. Lower the cooking plate and top ring; crack an egg into the egg plate and pierce to break the

yolk. Sprinkle some sea salt and pepper on the egg and top with the other muffin half.

3. Close the cover and cook for 4 to 5 minutes or until the egg is cooked through. Gently slide the egg plate out and remove the sandwich with a rubber spatula.

★ Serving Suggestion:Serve with a side of fresh tomato slices or a small cup of fruit.
★ Variation Tip:Replace the Havarti cheese with Swiss cheese or add some sliced mushrooms for an extra flavor boost.

NUTRITION FACTS:

Calories: 320 Fat: 15g Carbs: 30g Protein: 16g Fiber: 3g Sodium: 550mg

VEGETARIAN BOCA SANDWICHWICH

PREPARATION TIME: 5 MINUTES | COOKING TIME: 5 MINUTES | SERVINGS: 1

INGREDIENTS

- 1 whole wheat thin sandwich bun, sliced
- 2 tsp. Dijon mustard
- 1 Boca burger patty
- 1 slice Swiss cheese
- 1 large egg, beaten
- 1 slice red onion
- 1 slice tomato

PREPARATION:

1. Preheat the breakfast sandwich maker.
2. Place half of the sandwich bun, cut-side up, inside the bottom tray of the sandwich maker.
3. Brush the sandwich bun with Dijon mustard.
4. Top the sandwich bun with the Boca burger patty and Swiss cheese.
5. Slide the egg tray into place and pour the beaten egg into it.

6. Place the second half of the sandwich bun on top of the egg.
7. Close the sandwich maker and cook for 4 to 5 minutes until the egg is cooked through.
8. Carefully rotate the egg tray out of the sandwich maker then open the sandwich maker.
9. Remove the top of the sandwich bun and top the sandwich with the red onion and tomato.
10. Replace the sandwich bun top and enjoy your sandwich.

★ Serving Suggestion:Serve with a side of potato chips or a small salad.
★ Variation Tip:Add some sliced avocado or sprouts for extra nutrients.

NUTRITION FACTS:

Calories: 380| Fat: 18g| Carbs: 35g |Protein: 20g |Fiber: 6g |Sodium: 600mg

AVOCADO AND MIXED VEGETABLE PANINI

PREPARATION TIME: 20 MINUTES | COOKING TIME: 20 MINUTES | SERVINGS: 4

INGREDIENTS

- 1 1/2 tablespoons butter or olive oil
- 1 minced shallot (onion or garlic works too)
- 8 ounces sliced baby Portobello mushrooms
- 1 cup cherry or grape tomatoes
- 2 cups chopped kale, stems removed
- salt to taste
- 2 avocados
- 8 pieces thick, sturdy wheat bread
- White cheese like Provolone or Mozzarella

- Olive oil

PREPARATION:

1. Put the butter in a big skillet and allow it to melt on medium heat. Put in the shallots and cook until they become translucent. Mix in the mushrooms, and cook until they start to brown. Then mix in the kale and tomatoes, and cook until the kale wilts, and the tomatoes are cooked through.

2. Mash the avocados using a fork. Spread the avocado on what's going to be the inside of each piece of bread. Then place a layer of cheese on half of the pieces of bread, then a layer of veggies, and finally another layer of cheese. Top with another piece of bread. Brush the top and bottom of the sandwich with olive oil.

3. Cook the Panini on medium heat for 4 to 5 minutes, flipping halfway through. The bread should be brown, and the cheese should be melted.

★ Serving Suggestion:Serve with a side of sweet potato fries or a bowl of soup.
★ Variation Tip:Add some slices of cucumber or roasted red peppers for additional flavor and texture.

NUTRITION FACTS:

Calories: 450 |Fat: 20g| Carbs: 50g| Protein: 15g |Fiber: 10g |Sodium: 650mg

SAUERKRAUT SANDWICH

PREPARATION TIME: 2 MINUTES | COOKING TIME: 5 MINUTES | SERVINGS: 1

INGREDIENTS

- 1 Hard roll, cut in half

- ½ cup Sauerkraut
- Sliced Bratwurst, cooked
- 2 oz. Swiss Cheese, shredded

PREPARATION:

1. Cut the hard roll in half.

2. On one-half place the sauerkraut, bratwurst, and cheese. Place the second half of the roll.

3. Place on the sandwich maker and press for 5 minutes.

4. Serve and enjoy!

★ Serving Suggestion:Serve with a side of pickles or potato salad.
★ Variation Tip:Add some mustard or ketchup for extra flavor.

NUTRITION FACTS:

Calories: 550 | Fat: 30g |Carbs: 35g Protein: 25g |Fiber: 5g |Sodium: 1200mg

VEGGIE & CHEESE MELT

PREPARATION TIME: 3 MINUTES | COOKING TIME: 5 MINUTES | SERVINGS: 1

INGREDIENTS

- 2 slices sour dough bread
- 1 tomato slice
- 1 Tbsp. finely chopped spinach
- 1 Tbsp. finely diced precooked asparagus
- A few fresh onion rings
- 1 slice white cheddar cheese
- 1 egg
- Sea salt and pepper

PREPARATION:

1. Place one slice of sour dough bread into the bottom ring of the breakfast sandwich maker. Place tomato, spinach, asparagus, onion and white cheddar cheese on top.

2. Lower the cooking plate and top ring; crack an egg into the egg plate and pierce to break the yolk. Season with sea salt and pepper. Top with the other slice of bread.

3. Close the cover and cook for 4 to 5 minutes or until the egg is cooked and the cheese is melted. Carefully remove the sandwich with a rubber spat

★ Serving Suggestion:Serve with a side of carrot sticks or a small bowl of fruit.
★ Variation Tip:Replace the white cheddar cheese with Swiss cheese or add some sliced mushrooms for an extra flavor boost.

NUTRITION FACTS:

Calories: 350 |Fat: 15g |Carbs: 40g| Protein: 18g |Fiber: 5g |Sodium: 500mg

LEMONY DELICIOUS SUMMER VEGETABLE PANINI

 **PREPARATION TIME: 20 MINUTES** **COOKING TIME: 4 MINUTES** **SERVINGS: 4**

INGREDIENTS

- 1 tablespoon olive oil
- 1 small onion, sliced
- 1 medium yellow squash, thinly sliced
- 1 medium zucchini, thinly sliced
- 1 red bell pepper, sliced
- 2 teaspoons lemon zest
- ¼ teaspoon salt
- 4 Ciabatta rolls or 4 pieces of focaccia
- 1/8 teaspoon ground black pepper
- 1 cup part-skim ricotta cheese
- 2 teaspoons lemon zest
- 1 ½ teaspoons lemon juice
- 1/8 teaspoon salt
- 1/8 teaspoon ground black pepper

PREPARATION:

1. Place the oil in a skillet and heat it on medium high heat. Cook the onions in the oil for about 3 to 4 seconds, until they start to soften. Mix in the squash, peppers and zucchini and cook for another 5 to 7 minutes. Mix in the first 2 teaspoons of lemon zest and 1/8 teaspoon of pepper and the ¼ teaspoon of salt. Remove the mixture from the heat and set aside in a bowl.

2. Mix the last 5 ingredients (ricotta cheese, 2 teaspoons lemon zest, 1 ½ teaspoons lemon juice, 1/8 teaspoon salt, 1/8 teaspoon ground black pepper) in a bowl.

3. Slice the rolls in half horizontally and place a layer of the ricotta mixture on the inside of each piece of bread.

4. Place the vegetable mixture on the bottom pieces of bread. Put the top pieces of bread on the vegetables, making sure the ricotta side is touching the vegetables.

5. Cook the Panini on medium high heat for 3 to 4 minutes, flipping halfway through. The bread should be brown, and the cheese should be melted.

★ Serving Suggestion:Serve with a side of arugula salad or a bowl of fresh fruit.
★ Variation Tip:Add some fresh basil leaves or grated Parmesan cheese for an extra flavor boost.

NUTRITION FACTS:

Calories: 400 |Fat: 15g |Carbs: 55g |Protein: 12g| Fiber: 5g |Sodium: 550mg

VEGGIE BURGERS

INGREDIENTS

- 1 (15-ounce) can black beans, drained
- 1 medium carrot, grated
- ½ medium onion, chopped
- 3 medium potatoes, half-boiled, peeled and grated
- 4 large scallions, chopped
- 1 cup corn, fresh
- ½ teaspoon garlic salt
- 2 tablespoons olive oil

PREPARATION:

1. Blend black beans with onion, scallions, corn, salt, and carrot in a food processor for 1 minute.

2. Make 3 equal-sized patties out of the mixture.

3. Heat a suitable skillet with olive oil over medium-high heat.

4. Sear the bean patties in the oil for 5 minutes per side.

5. Preheat your Hamilton Beach Breakfast Sandwich Maker until the PREHEAT light turns green.

6. Lift the top cover, ring, and cooking plate.

7. Add ⅙ of the grated potato to the bottom tray of the sandwich maker.

8. Lower the cooking plate and top rings, then place a bean patty on top.

9. Add ⅙ of the grated potatoes on top and drizzle oil.

10. Cover the top hood and let the burger cook for 5 minutes.

11. Rotate the handle of the cooking plate clockwise until it stops.

12. Lift the hood, the rings, and transfer the burger to a plate.

13. Repeat the same steps with the remaining ingredients..

★ Serving Suggestion: Serve with a cauliflower bacon salad on the side.
★ Variation Tip: Add a layer of sliced bell peppers for a different taste.

 NUTRITION FACTS:

Calories 237 | Fat 19g | Sodium 518mg | Carbs 7g | Fiber 1.5g | Sugar 3.4g | Protein 12g

CORN BOWL WITH TOMATO, BACON, AND CHEESE

INGREDIENTS

- 1 Corn Tortilla
- 1 tbsp chopped Tomatoes
- 2 Basil Slices, chopped
- 1 ounce shredded Cheddar Cheese
- 2 Bacon Slices, chopped

PREPARATION:

1. Preheat the sandwich maker and grease it with some cooking spray.

2. Add the corn tortilla to the bottom ring, and press it well inside to make it look like a bowl.

3. Add the rest of the ingredients inside.

4. Close the unit and cook for 3 ½ minutes.

5. Lift up to open and carefully transfer to a plate.

6. Serve and enjoy!

★ Serving Suggestion: Serve with a side of ranch dressing or a dollop of sour cream.
★ Variation Tip: Replace the cheddar cheese with Monterey Jack cheese or add some sliced jalapeños for an extra kick.

 NUTRITION FACTS:

Calories 262 | Total Fats 16.4g | Carbs 13g | Protein 16g | Fiber 1.9g

EASY HAM AND SCRAMBLED EGG

 **PREPARATION TIME: 3 MINUTES**   **COOKING TIME: 5 MINUTES**   **SERVINGS: 1**

INGREDIENTS

- 2 slices whole grain bread
- 2 slices deli ham
- 1 slice Swiss cheese
- 1 large egg
- 2 teaspoons heavy cream
- 1 teaspoon chopped chives

PREPARATION:

1. Preheat the breakfast sandwich maker.

2. Place one slice of bread in the bottom tray of the sandwich maker.

3. Arrange the slices of ham on top of the bread and top with the slice of Swiss cheese.

4. Beat together the egg, heavy cream and chives in a small bowl.

5. Slide the egg tray into place over the cheese and pour the beaten egg mixture into the tray.

6. Top the egg mixture with the remaining slice of bread.

7. Close the sandwich maker and cook for 4 to 5 minutes until the egg is cooked through.

8. Carefully rotate the egg tray out of the sandwich maker then open the sandwich maker and enjoy your sandwich.

⭐ Serving Suggestion:Serve with a side of fresh fruit or a small serving of hash browns.

⭐ Variation Tip:Replace the white cheddar cheese with Swiss cheese or add some sliced mushrooms for an extra flavor boos

 **NUTRITION FACTS:**

Calories: 380 | Fat: 18g Carbs: 30g | Protein: 20g | Fiber: 5g | Sodium: 700mg

PORTABELLA AND SPINACH CROISSANT

PREPARATION TIME: 7 MINUTES   **COOKING TIME: 5 MINUTES**   **SERVINGS: 1**

INGREDIENTS

- 1 croissant, sliced
- 1 tsp. olive oil
- 1 cup baby spinach
- 1 tbsp. grated parmesan cheese
- 1 clove garlic, minced
- 1 portabella mushroom cap
- Salt and pepper to taste
- 1 large egg

PREPARATION:

1. Heat the olive oil in a small skillet over medium heat. Stir in the garlic and cook for 1 minute.

2. Add the spinach and cook for 2 minutes, stirring, until just wilted. Remove from heat and stir in the parmesan cheese.

3. Preheat the breakfast sandwich maker. Place half of the croissant, cut-side up, inside the bottom tray of the sandwich maker.

4. Top the croissant with the spinach mixture and the portabella mushroom cap. Sprinkle the mushroom with salt and pepper to taste.

5. Slide the egg tray into place and crack the egg into it. Use a fork to stir the egg, just breaking the yolk.

6. Place the second half of the croissant on top of the egg.

7. Close the sandwich maker and cook for 4 to 5 minutes until the egg is cooked through.

8. Carefully rotate the egg tray out of the sandwich maker then open the sandwich maker to enjoy your sandwich.

★ Serving Suggestion:Serve with a side of sliced tomatoes or a few cucumber spears.

★ Variation Tip:Replace the parmesan cheese with feta cheese or add some sliced onions to the spinach mixture.

NUTRITION FACTS:

Calories: 420 | Fat: 22g | Carbs: 35g | Protein: 18g | Fiber: 4g | Sodium: 580mg

GARLIC BLACK BEAN AND TOMATO BURGERS

PREPARATION TIME: 15 MINUTES

COOKING TIME: 15 MINUTES

SERVINGS: 4

INGREDIENTS

- 1 (14-ounce) can black beans, well-drained
- 2 tablespoons olive oil
- 2 slices bread, crumbled
- ½ medium onion, chopped
- ½ teaspoon seasoned salt
- 1 teaspoon garlic powder
- 1 teaspoon onion powder
- 1 dash black pepper
- 1 dash kosher salt
- ½ cup all-purpose flour
- ½ medium red onion, sliced
- 2 medium red heirloom tomatoes, sliced
- 6 leaves butter lettuce
- 4 buns, split

PREPARATION:

1. Blend black beans, crumbled bread, onion, salt, garlic powder, onion powder in a food processor for 1 minute.

2. Set a suitable skillet with olive oil over medium-high heat.

3. Make 4 equal-sized patties out of this bean mixture.

4. Sear the bean patties in the oil for 5 minutes per side.

5. Preheat your Hamilton Beach Breakfast Sandwich Maker until PREHEAT light gets green.

6. Lift the top cover, ring, and cooking plate.

7. Place half of a bun, cut-side up, inside the bottom tray of the sandwich maker.

8. Now lower the cooking plate and top rings, then place a patty, a lettuce leaf, an onion slice and a tomato slice on top.

9. Place the other top half of the bun on top.

10. Cover the top hood, and let the burger cook for 5 minutes.

11. Rotate the handle of the cooking plate clockwise until it stops.

12. Lift the hood, the rings and transfer the burger to a plate.

13. Repeat the same steps with the remaining ingredients.

★ Serving Suggestion:Serve the sandwich with crispy zucchini fries on the side.

★ Variation Tip:Add a layer of pickled onions for a change of taste.

NUTRITION FACTS:

Calories 229 | Fat 1.9 | Sodium 567mg| Carbs 1.9g | Fiber 0.4g | Sugar 0.6g | Protein 11.8g

AVOCADO AND MUSHROOM BURGER

INGREDIENTS

- 4 Portobello mushrooms, cut in half horizontally
- 1 medium onion, cut into slices
- 3 tablespoons olive oil
- ¾ teaspoon salt
- ½ teaspoon black pepper
- 1 avocado, peeled and sliced
- 2 tablespoons yogurt
- ½ teaspoon garlic, minced
- 4 hamburger buns, split in half
- 4 jarred roasted red peppers

PREPARATION:

1. Blend mushroom, onion, salt, black pepper, avocado, yoghurt, and garlic in a food processor for 1 minute.

2. Set a suitable skillet with olive oil over medium-high heat.

3. Make 4 equal-sized patties out of the mushroom mixture.

4. Sear the mushroom patties in the oil for 5 minutes per side.

5. Preheat your Hamilton Beach Breakfast Sandwich Maker until PREHEAT light gets green.

6. Lift the top cover, ring, and cooking plate.

7. Place half of a bun, cut-side up, inside the bottom tray of the sandwich maker.

8. Now lower the cooking plate and top rings then place a patty and red pepper on top.

9. Place the other top half of the bun on top.

10. Cover the top hood, and let the burger cook for 5 minutes.

11. Rotate the handle of the cooking plate clockwise until it stops.

12. Lift the hood, the rings and transfer the burger to a plate.

13. Repeat the same steps with the remaining ingredients.

★ Serving Suggestion:Serve the sandwich with crispy carrot chips on the side.

★ Variation Tip:You can add a lettuce leaf to the filling as well

 **NUTRITION FACTS:**

Calories 282 | Fat 15g | Sodium 526mg | Carbs 20g | Fiber 0.6g | Sugar 3.3g | Protein 16g

AVOCADO, CUCUMBER, AND BROCCOLI SANDWICH

INGREDIENTS

- 4 slices thin-sliced bread, cut into 4-inch rounds
- ½ avocado, peeled and sliced
- ⅛ teaspoon kosher salt
- 2 tablespoons plain hummus
- 8 slices tomato
- 8 slices cucumber
- ½ cup broccoli sprouts

PREPARATION:

1. Preheat your Hamilton Beach Breakfast Sandwich Maker until the PREHEAT light turns green.

2. Lift the top cover, ring, and cooking plate.

3. Place a bread slice in the bottom tray of the sandwich maker.

4. Spread ½ of the hummus, salt, avocado, tomato, cucumber, and broccoli sprouts, then place another bread slice on top.

5. Lower the cooking plate and top rings.

86

6. Place another bread slice on top.

7. Cover the top hood and let the sandwich cook for 5 minutes.

8. Rotate the handle of the cooking plate clockwise until it stops.

9. Lift the hood, the rings, and transfer the sandwich to a plate.

10. Repeat the same steps with the remaining ingredients.

★ Serving Suggestion: Serve with a broccoli salad on the side.

★ Variation Tip: Add a layer of sliced bell peppers for a different taste.

NUTRITION FACTS:

Calories 113 | Fat 3g | Sodium 152mg | Carbs 20g | Fiber 3g | Sugar 1.1g | Protein 3.5g

GARLIC BUFFALO CHICKPEAS BURGERS

PREPARATION TIME: 15 MINUTES | COOKING TIME: 12 MINUTES | SERVINGS: 4

INGREDIENTS

- 1 teaspoon canola oil
- ¼ cup chopped onion
- 1 garlic clove, minced
- 1 ½ cups canned chickpeas, drained
- 3 tablespoons Frank's Red Hot Sauce
- 1 tablespoon non-dairy butter
- ¼ teaspoon granulated onion
- 4 hamburger buns, split in half

PREPARATION:

1. Sauté chickpeas with oil, onion, garlic, red hot sauce, granulated onion, and butter in a skillet for 7 minutes.

2. Preheat your Hamilton Beach Breakfast Sandwich Maker until the PREHEAT light turns green.

3. Lift the top cover, ring, and cooking plate.

4. Place half of a bun, cut-side up, in the bottom tray of the sandwich maker.

5. Spread ¼ of the chickpeas over the bun.

6. Lower the cooking plate and top rings.

7. Place the other top half of the bun on top.

8. Cover the top hood and let the burger cook for 5 minutes.

9. Rotate the handle of the cooking plate clockwise until it stops.

10. Lift the hood, the rings, and transfer the burger to a plate.

11. Repeat the same steps with the remaining ingredients.

★ Serving Suggestion: Serve with crispy fries on the side.

★ Variation Tip: Add a layer of spicy mayo and pickled veggies for a different taste.

NUTRITION FACTS:

Calories 282 | Fat 15g | Sodium 526mg | Carbs 20g | Fiber 0.6g | Sugar 3.3g | Protein 16g

PORTABELLA AND SPINACH CROISSANT

PREPARATION TIME: 15 MINUTES | COOKING TIME: 7 MINUTES | SERVINGS: 1

INGREDIENTS

- 2 slices multigrain bread, cut in 4-inch circle
- 1 large egg, beaten
- 2 tablespoons plain nonfat yogurt

- ¼ teaspoon Dijon mustard
- ½ cup baby spinach
- 1 tablespoon minced yellow onion
- 1 teaspoon olive oil

PREPARATION:

1. Heat the oil in a suitable skillet over medium heat. Add the onion and spinach and stir well.
2. Cook for approximately 2 minutes, stirring, until the spinach is just wilted. Set aside.
3. Preheat your Hamilton Beach Breakfast Sandwich Maker.
4. Lift the top cover, ring, and cooking plate.
5. Place one bread slice in the sandwich maker.
6. Whisk together the yogurt and mustard in a small bowl, then brush over the piece of bread.
7. Top the bread with the cooked spinach and onion mixture.
8. Now lower the cooking plate and top rings, then pour in the egg.
9. Add the other circle of the bread on top.
10. Cover the top hood, and let the sandwich cook for 5 minutes.
11. When finished cooking, rotate the handle of the cooking plate clockwise until it stops.
12. Lift the hood, the rings and transfer the sandwich to a plate.

⭐ Serving Suggestion: Serve the sandwich with coleslaw and your favorite sauce on the side.
⭐ Variation Tip: Add some additional dried herbs to the filling.

NUTRITION FACTS:

Calories 305 | Fat 12.7g | Sodium 227mg | Carbs 26.1g | Fiber 1.4g | Sugar 0.9g | Protein 35.2g

EGG AND CHEESE SEED BAGEL

PREPARATION TIME: 15 MINUTES | COOKING TIME: 5 MINUTES | SERVINGS: 1

INGREDIENTS

- 1 poppy seed bagel, sliced
- 1-ounce goat cheese
- 1 large egg
- 1 teaspoon chopped chives
- Salt and black pepper to taste

PREPARATION:

1. Preheat your Hamilton Beach Breakfast Sandwich Maker.
2. Lift the top cover, ring, and cooking plate.
3. Place the lower half of the bagel in the sandwich maker.
4. Layer the goat cheese on top of the bagel.
5. Beat the egg with chopped chives, salt and pepper.
6. Now lower the cooking plate and top rings, then pour in the egg mixture.
7. Place the other top half of the bagel on top.
8. Cover the top hood, and let the sandwich cook for 5 minutes.
9. When finished cooking, rotate the handle of the cooking plate clockwise until it stops.
10. Lift the hood, the rings and transfer the sandwich to a plate.·

⭐ Serving Suggestion: Serve the sandwich with your favorite sauce on the side.
⭐ Variation Tip: You can add a lettuce leave to the filling as well.

NUTRITION FACTS:

Calories 354 | Fat 7.9g | Sodium 704mg | Carbs 6g | Fiber 3.6g | Sugar 6g | Protein 18g

EGG WHITES AND CHEESE ON CIABATTA

INGREDIENTS

- 1 ciabatta sandwich bun, sliced
- 1 teaspoon unsalted butter
- 1 slice mozzarella cheese
- 2 large egg whites
- 1 tablespoon skim milk
- 1 garlic clove, minced
- 1 teaspoon chopped chives
- ⅛ teaspoon dried Italian seasoning

PREPARATION:

1. Preheat your Hamilton Beach Breakfast Sandwich Maker.

2. Lift the top cover, ring, and cooking plate.

3. Place the lower half of the bun in the sandwich maker.

4. Spread the butter on the ciabatta bun. Top with the slice of mozzarella cheese.

5. Whisk together the egg whites, milk, garlic, chives and Italian seasoning.

6. Now lower the cooking plate and top rings, then pour in the egg.

7. Place the other top half of the bun on top.

8. Cover the top hood, and let the sandwich cook for 5 minutes.

9. When finished cooking, rotate the handle of the cooking plate clockwise until it stops.

10. Lift the hood, the rings and transfer the sandwich to a plate.

★ Serving Suggestion: Serve the sandwich with coleslaw and your favorite sauce on the side.

★ Variation Tip: Add some additional ground black pepper to the filling.

 **NUTRITION FACTS:**

Calories 545 | Fat 36g | Sodium 272mg | Carbs 41g | Fiber 0.2g | Sugar 0.1g | Protein 42.5g

MEXICAN GLUTEN-FREE PORK SANDWICH

PREPARATION TIME: 5 MINUTES | **COOKING TIME: 4 MINUTES** | **SERVINGS: 1**

INGREDIENTS

- 2 Corn Tortillas
- 2 ounces pulled Pork
- 2 tsp Salsa
- ½ tbsp Beans
- 1 tsp Corn
- 1 Tomato Slice, chopped
- 2 tsp Red Onion
- 2 tbsp shredded Cheddar Cheese

PREPARATION:

1. Preheat the sandwich maker and grease it with some cooking spray.
2. Cut the corn tortillas into 4-inch circles to fit inside the unit.
3. Place one tortilla to the bottom ring and place the pork on top.
4. Add the salsa, corn, beans, onion, and tomato, and top with the shredded cheese.
5. Lower the top ring and add the second corn tortilla.
6. Close and cook for 3-4 minutes.
7. Rotate clockwise and open carefully.
8. Transfer to a plate.
9. Serve and enjoy!

★ Serving Suggestion:Serve with a side of guacamole.

★ Variation Tip:Add some chopped jalapenos for an extra kick.

NUTRITION FACTS:

Calories 360 | Total Fats 25g | Carbs 21g | Protein 24g | Fiber 5g

ALMOND PANCAKE WITH EGG AND PROSCIUTTO

PREPARATION TIME: 5 MINUTES | **COOKING TIME: 4 MINUTES** | **SERVINGS: 1**

INGREDIENTS

- 2 4-inch Almond Flour Pancakes, fresh or frozen
- 1 Egg
- 1 ounce chopped Prosciutto
- 1 ounce shredded Cheddar
- Salt and Pepper, to taste

PREPARATION:

1. Preheat the sandwich maker and grease it with some cooking spray.
2. Add one pancake to the bottom ring and top it with prosciutto and cheddar.
3. Lower the top ring and cooking plate, and crack the egg into it. Season with salt and pepper.
4. Add the second pancake on top and close the unit.

5. Cook for 3 minutes or 4 if using frozen pancakes.

6. Open carefully and transfer to a plate.

7. Serve and enjoy!

★ Serving Suggestion:Serve with a side of fresh fruit salad.

★ Variation Tip:You could add some sliced tomatoes or spinach for extra nutrients.

 **NUTRITION FACTS:**

Calories 430 | Total Fats 34.5g | Carbs 5.8g | Protein 25g | Fiber: 1.3g

GLUTEN FREE SMOKED SALMON AND CREAM CHEESE SANDWICH

 PREPARATION TIME: 5 MINUTES COOKING TIME: 3 MINUTES  SERVINGS: 1

INGREDIENTS

- 1 ounce Smoked Salmon
- 1 tbsp Cream Cheese
- 1 ounce shredded Mozzarella
- 2 gluten-free Bread Slices

PREPARATION:

1. Preheat the sandwich maker and grease it with some cooking spray.

2. Cut the bread slices into circles that can fit inside the appliance.

3. When the green light appears, add one bread slice to the bottom ring.

4. Add half of the cream cheese and lightly spread it.

5. Add the smoked salmon and mozzarella on top.

6. Lower the top ring.

7. Spread the remaining cream cheese over the second bread slice.

8. Place the bread slice on top, with the cream cheese down.

9. Close the unit and cook for 3 minutes.

10. Rotate clockwise to open.

11. Serve and enjoy!

★ Serving Suggestion:Serve with a side of cucumber slices.

★ Variation Tip:Add some capers for an extra flavor boost.

 **NUTRITION FACTS:**

Calories 348 | Total Fats 14.6g | Carbs 39g | Protein 15g | Fiber: 5g

AVOCADO SANDWICH WITH EGG, HAM AND CHEESE

 PREPARATION TIME: 5 MINUTES  COOKING TIME: 4 MINUTES  SERVINGS: 1

INGREDIENTS

- 4 Large Avocado Slices
- 1 Egg
- 1 Ham Slice
- 1 slice American Cheese
- Salt and Pepper, to taste

PREPARATION:

1. Preheat the sandwich maker until the green light appears and grease it with cooking spray.

2. Arrange two of the avocado slices on the bottom ring.

3. Place the ham and cheese on top.

4. Lower the cooking plate and crack the egg into it. Season with salt and pepper.

5. Top with the remaining avocado slices.

6. Close the sandwich maker and cook for 4 minutes.

7. Side out and rotate clockwise. Open and transfer the sandwich with a spatula, very carefully, as you are using avocado slices, not bread.

8. Serve and enjoy!

★ Serving Suggestion:Pair with a small side of fresh tomato slices.

★ Variation Tip:Replace the American cheese with Swiss cheese for a different flavor.

 **NUTRITION FACTS:**

Calories 580 | Total Fats 44g | Carbs 21g | Protein 28g| Fiber: 12g

CORNBREAD AND EGG SANDWICH

INGREDIENTS

- 2 corn-only Cornbread Slices
- 1 Egg
- 1 tbsp shredded Cheddar
- 1 tsp cooked and crumbled Bacon

PREPARATION:

1. Preheat the unit and grease it with some cooking spray.

2. Cut the cornbread slices into rounds so they

---

can fit inside the unit, and place one on top of the bottom ring.

3. Add the cheddar and bacon.

4. Whisk the egg a bit, lower the cooking plate, and add it to it.

5. Place the second cornbread slice on top.

6. Close the sandwich maker and cook for 4 minutes.

7. Slide out and open the lid carefully.

8. Transfer to a plate and enjoy!

★ Serving Suggestion:Serve with a side of fresh fruit.

★ Variation Tip:Add some sliced tomatoes or spinach for added nutrients.

 **NUTRITION FACTS:**

Calories 320 | Total Fats 17g | Carbs 24g | Protein 12g| Fiber: 4g

ALMOND FLOUR WAFFLE AND SAUSAGE SANDWICH

INGREDIENTS

- 2 Almond Flour Waffles
- 1 Frozen Sausage Pattie
- 1 slice American Cheese
- 2 Red Onion Rings
- 2 Tomato Slices

PREPARATION:

1. Preheat the sandwich maker until the green light appears and grease the unit with cooking spray.

2. Add one waffle to the bottom ring and top with the sausage pattie.

3. Add the tomato slices and red onion over, and place the cheese on top.

4. Lower the top ring and add the second waffle.

5. Close the unit and cook for 4 minutes.

6. Rotate clockwise and open.

7. Serve and enjoy!

★ Serving Suggestion:Pair with a small side of hash browns.

★ Variation Tip:Use a different type of cheese, like cheddar or Swiss, for a change of flavor.

 **NUTRITION FACTS:**

Calories 345 | Total Fats 28g | Carbs 14g | Protein 20g| Fiber: 7g

CORN BOWL WITH TOMATO, BACON, AND CHEESE

| PREPARATION TIME: 5 MINUTES | COOKING TIME: 3 MINUTES | SERVINGS: 1 |

INGREDIENTS

- 1 Corn Tortilla
- 1 tbsp chopped Tomatoes
- 2 Basil Slices, chopped
- 1 ounce shredded Cheddar Cheese
- 2 Bacon Slices, chopped

PREPARATION:

1. Preheat the sandwich maker and grease it with some cooking spray.

2. Add the corn tortilla to the bottom ring, and press it well inside to make it look like a bowl.

3. Add the rest of the ingredients inside.

4. Close the unit and cook for 3 ½ minutes.

5. Lift up to open and carefully transfer to a plate.

6. Serve and enjoy!

★ Serving Suggestion:Serve with a side of ranch dressing for dipping.

★ Variation Tip:Add some sliced jalapeños for an extra kick.

 **NUTRITION FACTS:**

Calories 262 | Total Fats 16.4g | Carbs 13g | Protein 16g| Fiber: 1.9g

GLUTEN-FREE CRISPY GRILLED CHEESE AND BACON SANDWICH

| PREPARATION TIME: 5 MINUTES | COOKING TIME: 3 MINUTES | SERVINGS: 1 |

INGREDIENTS

- 1 ounce Bacon, chopped
- 1 ounce shredded Cheddar
- 1 ounce shredded Gouda
- 2 tsp Butter
- 2 Gluten-Free Bread

PREPARATION:

1. Preheat the unit until the green light appears. Grease with some cooking spray.

2. Spread the butter over the bread slices, and cut them to make them fit inside the unit.

3. Place one bread slice on top of the bottom ring, with the butter-side down.

4. Top with the cheese and bacon.

5. Lower the top ring and add the second slice

of bread, with the butter-side up.

6. Close the lid and cook for 3 ½ minutes.

7. Rotate clockwise, open, and transfer to a plate

8. Serve and enjoy!

★ Serving Suggestion:Serve with a cup of tomato soup.

★ Variation Tip:Add some sliced tomatoes or spinach for an extra boost of nutrients.

 **NUTRITION FACTS:**

Calories 430 | Total Fats 22g | Carbs 39g | Protein 20g | Fiber: 5g

MUSHROOMS AND CRAB MELT SANDWICH

 PREPARATION TIME: 15 MINUTES

 COOKING TIME: 5 MINUTES

 SERVINGS: 4

INGREDIENTS

- 4 large Portobello mushrooms cap, split in half
- Spray coconut oil
- Salt and pepper to taste
- 8 ounces lump crab meat
- 3 tablespoons mayonnaise
- ½ teaspoon Worcestershire sauce
- ½ teaspoon old bay seasoning
- ¼ teaspoon sea salt
- Dash black pepper
- Dash cayenne pepper
- ½ cup finely shredded cheddar cheese
- 1 tablespoon chopped parsley
- 4 green onions sliced

PREPARATION:

1. Mix crab meat with mayonnaise, Worcestershire sauce, old bay seasoning, black pepper, salt, cayenne pepper, parsley and onion.
2. Preheat your Hamilton Beach Breakfast Sandwich Maker until PREHEAT light gets green.
3. Lift the top cover, ring, and cooking plate.
4. Place one circle of the mushroom in the sandwich maker.
5. Top it with cheese and ¼ of the crab mixture.
6. lower the cooking plate and top rings.
7. Add the other circle of the mushroom on top.
8. Cover the top hood, and let the sandwich cook for 5 minutes.
9. Rotate the handle of the cooking plate clockwise until it stops.
10. Lift the hood, the rings and transfer the sandwich to a plate.
11. Repeat the same with the remaining ingredients.

★ Serving Suggestion: Serve the sandwich with crispy bacon and your favorite keto sauce on the side.
★ Variation Tip: Add a layer of pickled onions for a change of taste.

 **NUTRITION FACTS:**

Calories 395 | Fat 9.5g | Sodium 655mg | Carbs 3.4g | Fiber 0.4g | Sugar 0.4g | Protein 28.3g

CHEDDAR AND CAULIFLOWER SANDWICH

 PREPARATION TIME: 15 MINUTES

 COOKING TIME: 5 MINUTES

 SERVINGS: 6

INGREDIENTS

- 1 head riced cauliflower cooked
- 1 egg, beaten
- 1 ½ cups cheddar cheese, grated
- 12 mozzarella Cheese, slices
- ⅛ teaspoon dried sage
- ⅛ teaspoon dried oregano

- dash teaspoon ground mustard seed
- dash teaspoon dried thyme
- ground black pepper
- butter for greasing
- fresh parsley for garnishing

PREPARATION:

1. At 350 degrees F, preheat your oven.

2. Blend cauliflower with egg, dried thyme, spices and grated cheese in a blender until smooth.

3. Line a suitable baking sheet with parchment paper and divide the cauliflower mixture into 3-4-inches equal rounds onto the baking sheet.

4. Bake the cauliflower circles for 5 minutes per side.

5. Preheat your Hamilton Beach Breakfast Sandwich Maker.

6. Lift the top cover, ring, and cooking plate.

7. Place one circle of the cauliflower bread in the sandwich maker.

8. Top it with 1 mozzarella cheese slice.

9. Now lower the cooking plate and top rings.

10. Add the other circle of the bread on top and brush it with butter.

11. Cover the top hood, and let the sandwich cook for 5 minutes.

12. When finished cooking, rotate the handle of the cooking plate clockwise until it stops.

13. Lift the hood, the rings and transfer the sandwich to a plate.

14. Garnish with parsley.

15. Repeat the same steps with remaining ingredients.

★ Serving Suggestion:Serve the sandwich with coleslaw and your favorite sauce on the side.

★ Variation Tip:You can add a lettuce leave to the filling as well.

 **NUTRITION FACTS:**

Calories 301 | Fat 5g | Sodium 340mg | Carbs 4.7g | Fiber 1.2g | Sugar 1.3g | Protein 15.3g

AVOCADO CHICKEN SANDWICH

PREPARATION TIME: 15 MINUTES | COOKING TIME: 5 MINUTES | SERVINGS: 2

INGREDIENTS

- ½ cup almond flour
- ¼ cup whey protein isolate
- 1 teaspoon xanthan gum
- ½ teaspoons baking powder
- ½ cup egg whites
- ½ avocado mashed
- 3 slices of tomato
- 2 slices cheese
- 4 ounces grilled chicken breast
- Salt and black pepper to taste

PREPARATION:

1. Mix almond flour with protein, xanthan gum, baking powder and egg whites in a 4-inch ramekin.

2. Cook this bread batter in the microwave for 1-2 minutes the slice into 2 equal sized slices.

3. Preheat your Hamilton Beach Breakfast Sandwich Maker.

4. Lift the top cover, ring, and cooking plate.

5. Place the lower half of the bread in the sandwich maker.

6. Now lower the cooking plate and top rings then place ½ of the fillings on top.

7. Add the other circle of the bread on top.

8. Cover the top hood, and let the sandwich cook for 5 minutes.

9. When finished cooking, rotate the handle of the cooking plate clockwise until it stops.

10. Lift the hood, the rings and transfer the sandwich to a plate.

11. Repeat the same steps with remaining ingredients.

★ Serving Suggestion:Serve the sandwich with crispy bacon and your favorite sauce on the side.

★ Variation Tip:Add some additional dried herbs to the filling.

NUTRITION FACTS:

Calories 361 | Fat 10g | Sodium 218mg | Carbs 6g | Fiber 10g | Sugar 30g | Protein 14g

HERBED CAULIFLOWER AND PORK SANDWICH

PREPARATION TIME: 15 MINUTES | COOKING TIME: 5 MINUTES | SERVINGS: 6

INGREDIENTS

- 1 head riced cauliflower cooked
- 1 egg beaten
- 1 ½ cups cheddar cheese grated
- 12 mozzarella Cheese, slices
- ⅛ teaspoon dried sage
- ⅛ teaspoon dried oregano
- dash teaspoon ground mustard seed
- dash teaspoon dried thyme
- ground black pepper
- 1 cup pulled barbecue pork
- butter for greasing
- fresh parsley for garnishing

PREPARATION:

1. At 350 degrees F, preheat your oven.

2. Blend cauliflower with egg, dried herbs, spices and grated cheese in a blender until smooth.

3. Line a suitable baking sheet with parchment paper and divide the cauliflower mixture into 3-4-

inches equal rounds onto the baking sheet.

4. Bake the cauliflower circles for 5 minutes per side.

5. Preheat your Hamilton Beach Breakfast Sandwich Maker.

6. Lift the top cover, ring, and cooking plate.

7. Place one circle of the cauliflower bread in the sandwich maker and top it with pork.

8. Top it with 1 mozzarella cheese slice.

9. Now lower the cooking plate and top rings.

10. Add the other circle of the bread on top and brush it with butter.

11. Cover the top hood, and let the sandwich cook for 5 minutes.

12. When finished cooking, rotate the handle of the cooking plate clockwise until it stops.

13. Lift the hood, the rings and transfer the sandwich to a plate.

14. Repeat the same steps with remaining ingredients.

15. Garnish with parsley.

★ Serving Suggestion:Serve the sandwich with coleslaw and your favorite sauce on the side.

★ Variation Tip:You can add a lettuce leave to the filling as well.

NUTRITION FACTS:

Calories 195 | Fat 3g | Sodium 355mg | Carbs 7.7g | Fiber 1g | Sugar 25g | Protein 1g

MAYO BEEF SANDWICH

PREPARATION TIME: 15 MINUTES | COOKING TIME: 17 MINUTES | SERVINGS: 1

INGREDIENTS

- ½ cup almond flour
- ¼ cup whey protein isolate

- 1 teaspoon xanthan gum
- ½ teaspoon baking powder
- ½ cup egg whites
- ¼ lb. ground beef
- 1 pinch salt
- 1 pinch ground black pepper
- ½ tablespoon butter
- ¼ onion, sliced
- 1 teaspoon mayonnaise
- 1 slices rye bread
- 1 slices sharp cheddar cheese

PREPARATION:

1. Mix almond flour with protein, xanthan gum, baking powder and egg whites in a 4-inch ramekin.

2. Cook this bread batter in the microwave for 1-2 minutes the slice into 2 equal-sized slices.

3. Mix beef with black pepper, salt, butter and onion in a food processor for 1 minute.

4. Make 1 patty out of this mixture.

5. Sear the patty in a skillet for 5 minutes per side.

6. Preheat your Hamilton Beach Breakfast Sandwich Maker until PREHEAT light gets green.

7. Lift the top cover, ring, and cooking plate.

8. Place one bread slice inside the bottom tray of the sandwich maker then spread 1 teaspoon mayonnaise on top.

9. Place a beef patty and a cheese slice on top of the mayo.

10. Now lower the cooking plate and top rings.

11. Place another bread slice on top.

12. Cover the top hood, and let the sandwich cook for 5 minutes.

13. Rotate the handle of the cooking plate clockwise until it stops.

14. Lift the hood, the rings and transfer the sandwich to a plate.

★ Serving Suggestion:Serve the sandwich with your favorite keto dip on the side.
★ Variation Tip:Add some additional black pepper to the filling.

NUTRITION FACTS:

Calories 361 | Fat 16g | Sodium 515mg | Carbs 9.3g | Fiber 0.1g | Sugar 18.2g | Protein 33.3g

AVOCADO AND CAULIFLOWER BAGEL SANDWICHES

PREPARATION TIME: 15 MINUTES | COOKING TIME: 15 MINUTES | SERVINGS: 2

INGREDIENTS

- 1 head cauliflower, cut into florets
- 2 eggs
- 2 tablespoons almond flour
- 1 tablespoon coconut flour
- ½ teaspoon garlic powder
- ¼ teaspoon fine sea salt
- ½ teaspoon poppy seeds
- 1 tablespoon sesame seeds
- 1 teaspoon dried minced garlic
- 1 tablespoon dried minced onion
- ½ teaspoon coarse sea salt
- 1 avocado, mashed
- 2 tablespoons mayonnaise
- ½ cup shredded cheddar

PREPARATION:

1. At 350 degrees F, preheat your oven.

2. Blend cauliflower with almond flour, coconut flour, eggs, garlic powder, sea salt, poppy seeds, garlic and onion in a food processor.

3. Line a suitable baking sheet with parchment paper and divide the cauliflower mixture into 3-4-inches equal rounds with a hole at the centre onto the baking sheet and drizzle seeds on top.

4. Bake the cauliflower circles for 10 minutes until golden brown.

5. Preheat your Hamilton Beach Breakfast Sandwich Maker until PREHEAT light gets green.

6. Lift the top cover, ring, and cooking plate.

7. Split the baked bagels in half.

8. Place one half of a bagel in the sandwich maker.

9. Now lower the cooking plate and top rings, then add ½ of cheddar, mayo and avocado.

10. Place the other top half of the bagel on top.

11. Cover the top hood, and let the sandwich cook for 5 minutes.

12. Rotate the handle of the cooking plate clockwise until it stops.

13. Lift the hood, the rings and transfer the sandwich to a plate.

14. Repeat the same steps with the remaining ingredients.

★ Serving Suggestion:Serve the sandwich with favorite keto smoothie on the side.
★ Serving Suggestion:Serve the sandwich with favorite keto smoothie on the side.

 **NUTRITION FACTS:**

Calories 245 | Fat 14g | Sodium 122mg | Carbs 8g | Fiber 1.2g | Sugar 12g | Protein 4.3g

HEARTY SCRAMBLED EGG SANDWICH

 PREPARATION TIME: 15 MINUTES COOKING TIME: 7 MINUTES  SERVINGS: 1

INGREDIENTS

- ½ cup almond flour
- ¼ cup whey protein isolate
- 1 teaspoon xanthan gum
- ½ teaspoon baking powder
- ½ cup egg whites
- 1 egg, scrambled
- 1 pinch salt
- 1 pinch black pepper

PREPARATION:

1. Mix almond flour with protein, xanthan gum, baking powder and egg whites in a 4-inch ramekin.

2. Cook this bread batter in the microwave for 1-2 minutes the slice into 2 equal-sized slices.

3. Preheat your Hamilton Beach Breakfast Sandwich Maker until PREHEAT light gets green.

4. Lift the top cover, ring, and cooking plate.

5. Place one slice of the bread in the sandwich maker.

6. Now lower the cooking plate and top rings then add scrambled egg, salt and black pepper.

7. Add the other circle of the bread on top.

8. Cover the top hood, and let the sandwich cook for 5 minutes.

9. Rotate the handle of the cooking plate clockwise until it stops.

10. Lift the hood, the rings and transfer the sandwich to a plate.

★ Serving Suggestion:Serve the sandwich with your favorite keto smoothie on the side.
★ Variation Tip:Add some additional cream to the filling.

 **NUTRITION FACTS:**

Calories 361 | Fat 16g | Sodium 515mg | Carbs 9.3g | Fiber 0.1g | Sugar 18.2g | Protein 33.3g

TOFU, HAM, AND CHEESE SANDWICH

INGREDIENTS

- ½ cup almond flour
- ¼ cup whey protein isolate
- 1 teaspoon xanthan gum
- ½ teaspoon baking powder
- ½ cup egg whites
- 2 tofu slices
- 1 slice ham
- 1 cheese slices

PREPARATION:

1. Set a non-stick pan on medium heat and sear the tofu slices for 3 minutes per side.

2. Mix almond flour with protein, xanthan gum, baking powder and egg whites in a 4-inch ramekin.

3. Cook this bread batter in the microwave for 1-2 minutes the slice into 2 equal-sized slices.

4. Preheat your Hamilton Beach Breakfast Sandwich Maker until PREHEAT light gets green.

5. Lift the top cover, ring, and cooking plate.

6. Place a bread slice in the sandwich maker.

7. Now lower the cooking plate and top rings then place tofu, ham and cheese on top.

8. Add the other circle of the bread on top.

9. Cover the top hood, and let the sandwich cook for 5 minutes.

10. Rotate the handle of the cooking plate clockwise until it stops.

11. Lift the hood, the rings and transfer the sandwich to a plate.

★ Serving Suggestion:Serve the sandwich with your favorite keto sauce on the side

★ Variation Tip:Add some additional dried herbs to the filling.

 **NUTRITION FACTS:**

Calories 361 | Fat 16g | Sodium 515mg | Carbs 9.3g |
Fiber 0.1g | Sugar 18.2g | Protein 33.3g

CUBAN BACON AND TOMATO SANDWICH

INGREDIENTS

- ½ cup almond flour
- ¼ cup whey protein isolate
- 1 teaspoon xanthan gum
- ½ teaspoons baking powder
- ½ cup egg whites
- 1 pepperoni slice
- 1 slice bacon
- ¼ cup pulled pork
- 1 cheese slices
- 1 slice tomatoes

PREPARATION:

1. Mix almond flour with protein, xanthan gum, baking powder and egg whites in a 4-inch ramekin.

2. Cook this bread batter in the microwave for 1-2 minutes the slice into 2 equal sized slices.

3. Preheat your Hamilton Beach Breakfast Sandwich Maker.

4. Lift the top cover, ring, and cooking plate.

5. Place the lower half of the bread in the sandwich maker.

6. Now lower the cooking plate and top rings then place ½ of the fillings on top.

7. Add the other circle of the bread on top.

8. Cover the top hood, and let the sandwich cook for 5 minutes.

9. When finished cooking, rotate the handle of the cooking plate clockwise until it stops.

10. Lift the hood, the rings and transfer the sandwich to a plate.

11. Repeat the same steps with remaining ingredients.

★ Serving Suggestion:Serve the sandwich with crispy bacon and your favorite sauce on the side.

★ Variation Tip:Add some additional ground black pepper to the filling.

NUTRITION FACTS:

Calories 405 | Fat 22.7g | Sodium 227mg | Carbs 6.1g | Fiber 1.4g | Sugar 0.9g | Protein 45.2g

KETO CHICKEN, CAULIFLOWER, AND CRANBERRY SANDWICH

PREPARATION TIME: 15 MINUTES | COOKING TIME: 5 MINUTES | SERVINGS: 1

INGREDIENTS

- 1 cauliflower head, riced cooked
- 1 egg beaten
- 1 ½ cups cheddar cheese, grated
- 12 mozzarella Cheese, slices
- ⅛ teaspoon dried sage
- ⅛ teaspoon dried oregano
- 1 dash teaspoon ground mustard seed
- 1 dash teaspoon dried thyme
- Black pepper, to taste
- Butter for greasing
- Parsley for garnishing
- 2 teaspoons of mayonnaise
- 2 tablespoons of dried cranberries
- 1 cup of cooked chicken
- 1 teaspoon of chopped parsley

PREPARATION:

1. At 350 degrees F, preheat your oven.

2. Blend cauliflower with egg, dried herbs, spices and grated cheese in a blender until smooth.

3. Line a suitable baking sheet with parchment paper and divide the cauliflower mixture into 3-4-inches equal rounds onto the baking sheet.

4. Bake the cauliflower circles for 5 minutes per side.

5. Preheat your Hamilton Beach Breakfast Sandwich Maker.

6. Lift the top cover, ring, and cooking plate.

7. Place one circle of the cauliflower bread in the sandwich maker.

8. Top it with 1 mozzarella cheese slice.

9. Now lower the cooking plate and top rings then place the remaining fillings.

10. Add the other circle of the bread on top and brush it with butter.

11. Cover the top hood, and let the sandwich cook for 5 minutes.

12. When finished cooking, rotate the handle of the cooking plate clockwise until it stops.

13. Lift the hood, the rings and transfer the sandwich to a plate.

14. Garnish with parsley.

★ Serving Suggestion:Serve the sandwich with your favorite sauce on the side.

★ Variation Tip:Add some additional dried herbs to the filling.

NUTRITION FACTS:

Calories 159 | Fat 3g | Sodium 277mg | Carbs 9g | Fiber 1g | Sugar 9g | Protein 2g

EGG, WATERCRESS, AND BEEF SANDWICH

INGREDIENTS

- 2 large egg
- ¼ teaspoon fresh basil, chopped
- ¼ teaspoon fresh Italian parsley, chopped
- black pepper, to taste
- ½ teaspoon grated lemon zest
- Salt, to taste
- 6 ounces freshly sliced rare roast beef
- 1 cup watercress

PREPARATION:

1. Beat egg with basil, black pepper, salt and parsley in a small bowl.

2. Set a pan with two 4-inches metal rings in it.

3. Pour half of the prepared egg mixture into each ring and cook for 1-2 minutes per side.

4. Preheat your Hamilton Beach Breakfast Sandwich Maker.

5. Lift the top cover, ring, and cooking plate.

6. Place one half of the egg in the sandwich maker.

7. Now lower the cooking plate and top rings then add remaining fillings.

8. Place the other top half of the egg circle on top.

9. Cover the top hood, and let the sandwich cook for 5 minutes.

10. When finished cooking, rotate the handle of the cooking plate clockwise until it stops.

11. Lift the hood, the rings and transfer the sandwich to a plate.

★ Serving Suggestion:Serve the sandwich with crispy bacon and your favorite sauce on the side.

★ Variation Tip:Add some additional dried herbs to the filling.

 **NUTRITION FACTS:**

Calories 203 | Fat 8.9g | Sodium 340mg | Carbs 7.2g | Fiber 1.2g | Sugar 11.3g | Protein 5.3g

CHICKEN AND AVOCADO PANINI

INGREDIENTS

- ½ cup almond flour
- ¼ cup whey protein isolate
- 1 teaspoon xanthan gum
- ½ teaspoons baking powder
- ½ cup egg whites
- 1 avocado, sliced
- 1 slice ham
- 1 chicken patty, cooked
- 1 cheese slices
- 1 slice tomatoes

PREPARATION:

1. Mix almond flour with protein, xanthan gum, baking powder and egg whites in a 4-inch ramekin.

2. Cook this bread batter in the microwave for 1-2 minutes the slice into 2 equal sized slices.

3. Preheat your Hamilton Beach Breakfast Sandwich Maker.

4. Lift the top cover, ring, and cooking plate.

5. Place the lower half of the bread in the sandwich maker.

6. Now lower the cooking plate and top rings, then place ½ of the fillings on top.

7. Add the other circle of the bread on top.

8. Cover the top hood, and let the sandwich cook for 5 minutes.

9. When finished cooking, rotate the handle of the cooking plate clockwise until it stops.

10. Lift the hood, the rings and transfer the sandwich to a plate.

11. Repeat the same steps with remaining ingredients.

★ Serving Suggestion:Serve the sandwich with crispy bacon and your favorite sauce on the side.

★ Variation Tip:You can add a lettuce leave to the filling as well.

 **NUTRITION FACTS:**

Calories 351 | Fat 19g | Sodium 412mg | Carbs 3g | Fiber 0.3g | Sugar 1g | Protein 23g

SPINACH, AVOCADO, AND CHEESE PANINI

 PREPARATION TIME: 15 MINUTES

 COOKING TIME: 5 MINUTES

 SERVINGS: 2

INGREDIENTS

- ½ cup almond flour
- ¼ cup whey protein isolate
- 1 teaspoon xanthan gum
- ½ teaspoons baking powder
- ½ cup egg whites
- 1 slice Colby jack cheese
- 6 leaves spinach
- 2 slices tomatoes
- ½ avocado sliced

PREPARATION:

1. Mix almond flour with protein, xanthan gum, baking powder and egg whites in a 4-inch ramekin.

2. Cook this bread batter in the microwave for 1-2 minutes the slice into 2 equal sized slices.

3. Preheat your Hamilton Beach Breakfast Sandwich Maker.

4. Lift the top cover, ring, and cooking plate.

5. Place the lower half of the bread in the sandwich maker.

6. Now lower the cooking plate and top rings then place ½ of the fillings on top.

7. Add the other circle of the bread on top.

8. Cover the top hood, and let the sandwich cook for 5 minutes.

9. When finished cooking, rotate the handle of the cooking plate clockwise until it stops.

10. Lift the hood, the rings and transfer the sandwich to a plate.

11. Repeat the same steps with remaining ingredients.

★ Serving Suggestion:Serve the sandwich with your favorite sauce on the side.

★ Variation Tip:Add some additional ground black pepper to the filling.

 **NUTRITION FACTS:**

Calories 248 | Fat 16g | Sodium 95mg | Carbs 8.4g | Fiber 0.3g | Sugar 10g | Protein 14.1g

MUSHROOM-CUCUMBER PANINI

 PREPARATION TIME: 15 MINUTES

 COOKING TIME: 5 MINUTES

 SERVINGS: 2

INGREDIENTS

- 4 Portobello mushroom caps, pressed
- 1 small seedless cucumber, sliced
- 4 ounces sliced black olives, drained
- 1 small onion, quartered
- 1 red bell pepper, chopped
- 1 green bell pepper, chopped
- ¼ cup Brianna's Real French Vinaigrette Dressing

PREPARATION:

1. Mix all cucumber and all the veggies in a bowl with the dressing.

2. Preheat your Hamilton Beach Breakfast Sandwich Maker.

3. Lift the top cover, ring, and cooking plate.

4. Place one circle of the mushroom in the sandwich maker.

5. Top it with ½ of the veggie mixture.

6. Now lower the cooking plate and top rings.

7. Add the other circle of the mushroom on top.

8. Cover the top hood, and let the sandwich cook for 5 minutes.

9. When finished cooking, rotate the handle of the cooking plate clockwise until it stops.

10. Lift the hood, the rings and transfer the sandwich to a plate.

11. Repeat the same with remaining ingredients.

★ Serving Suggestion:Serve the sandwich with crispy bacon and your favorite sauce on the side.

★ Variation Tip:You can add a lettuce leave to the filling as well.

NUTRITION FACTS:

Calories 395 | Fat 9.5g | Sodium 655mg | Carbs 3.4g | Fiber 0.4g | Sugar 0.4g | Protein 28.3g

KETO SAUSAGE AND CHEDDAR SANDWICH

 PREPARATION TIME: 15 MINUTES
 COOKING TIME: 9 MINUTES
 SERVINGS: 1

INGREDIENTS

- 2 large egg
- ¼ teaspoon fresh basil, chopped
- ¼ teaspoon fresh Italian parsley, chopped
- Salt, to taste
- black pepper, to taste
- 1 (1.2-ounces) fully cooked turkey sausage patty
- 1 (0.5-ounces) slice cracker-cuts sharp Cheddar cheese

PREPARATION:

1. Beat egg with basil, black pepper, salt and parsley in a small bowl.

2. Set a pan with two 4-inches metal rings in it.

3. Pour half of the prepared egg mixture into each ring and cook for 1-2 minutes per side.

4. Preheat your Hamilton Beach Breakfast Sandwich Maker.

5. Lift the top cover, ring, and cooking plate.

6. Place one half of the egg in the sandwich maker.

7. Now lower the cooking plate and top rings then add sausage patty and cheddar cheese.

8. Place the other top half of the egg circle on top.

9. Cover the top hood, and let the sandwich cook for 5 minutes.

10. When finished cooking, rotate the handle of the cooking plate clockwise until it stops.

11. Lift the hood, the rings and transfer the sandwich to a plate.

★ Serving Suggestion:Serve the sandwich with crispy bacon and your favorite sauce on the side.

★ Variation Tip:You can add a lettuce leave to the filling as well.

NUTRITION FACTS:

Calories 245 | Fat 14g | Sodium 122mg | Carbs 8g | Fiber 1.2g | Sugar 12g | Protein 4.3g

KETO CORN BLUE CORN PORK SANDWICH

INGREDIENTS

- 2 Corn Tortillas
- 2 ounces pulled Pork
- 2 tsp Salsa
- ½ tbsp Beans
- 1 tsp Corn
- 1 Tomato Slice, chopped
- 2 tsp Red Onion
- 2 tbsp shredded Cheddar Cheese

PREPARATION:

1. Preheat the sandwich maker and grease it with some cooking spray.

2. Cut the corn tortillas into 4-inch circles to fit inside the unit.

3. Place one tortilla to the bottom ring and place the pork on top.

4. Add the salsa, corn, beans, onion, and tomato, and top with the shredded cheese.

5. Lower the top ring and add the second corn tortilla.

6. Close and cook for 3 – 4 minutes.

7. Rotate clockwise and open carefully.

8. Transfer to a plate.

9. Serve and enjoy!

★ Serving Suggestion: Serve with a side of guacamole.

★ Variation Tip:Add some sliced jalapeños for an extra kick.

 **NUTRITION FACTS:**

Calories 360 | Total Fats 25g | Carbs 21g | Protein 24g | Fiber: 5g

CHOCOLATE DONUT DESSERT SANDWICH

PREPARATION TIME: 3 MINUTES

COOKING TIME: 5 MINUTES

SERVINGS: 1

INGREDIENTS

- 1 chocolate-frosted glazed donut, sliced in half
- 2 tbsp. chocolate hazelnut spread
- 1 ounce cream cheese
- ½ cup sliced strawberries

PREPARATION:

1. Divide the two tablespoons chocolate hazelnut spread between the donut halves, spreading it evenly along the cut edges.

2. Preheat the breakfast sandwich maker.

3. Place half of the donut inside the bottom tray of the sandwich maker.

4. Top the donut with cream cheese and strawberries.

5. Place the second half of the donut on top of the strawberries.

6. Close the sandwich maker and cook for 4 to 5 minutes until heated through.

7. Carefully open the sandwich maker and enjoy your sandwich.

★ Serving Suggestion:Serve with a side of vanilla ice cream.

★ Variation Tip:Replace the strawberries with raspberries or blueberries.

NUTRITION FACTS:

Calories: 550 | Total Fat: 30g | Saturated Fat: 15g | Trans Fat: 0g | Cholesterol: 60mg | Sodium: 250mg | Total Carbohydrate: 65g | Dietary Fiber: 3g | Sugars: 40g | Protein: 7g

THE ULTIMATE 4-MINUTE CHEESEBURGER

PREPARATION TIME: 5 MINUTES

COOKING TIME: 4 MINUTES

SERVINGS: 1

INGREDIENTS

- 1 frozen Beef Patty
- 1 small Hamburger Bun
- 1 slice American Cheese
- 1 ounce cooked and crumbled Bacon
- 1 tsp Pickle Relish
- 2 Tomato Slices
- 1 tsp Dijon Mustard

PREPARATION:

1. Preheat the sandwich maker and grease it with some cooking spray.

2. Cut the bun in half and place one on top of the bottom ring.

3. Add the patty on top and brush with the mustard.

4. Top with bacon, pickle relish, and tomato slices.

5. Place the cheese on top.

6. Lower the top ring and add the second bun half.

7. Close the unit and cook for 4 minutes.

8. Open carefully and transfer to a plate.

9. Serve and enjoy!

★ Serving Suggestion:Serve with a side of fries or onion rings.

★ Variation Tip:Use a different type of cheese, such as cheddar or Swiss.

 **NUTRITION FACTS:**

Calories 480 | Total Fats 31g | Carbs 24g | Protein 28g| Fiber 2g

HERBED OMELET WITH CREAM CHEESE AND CHEDDAR

 PREPARATION TIME: 5 MINUTES COOKING TIME: 4 MINUTES SERVINGS: 1

INGREDIENTS

- 1 ounce Shredded Cheddar
- 2 Eggs
- ¼ tsp Garlic Powder
- 2 tsp Cream Cheese
- 1 tsp chopped Parsley
- 1 tsp chopped Cilantro
- ½ tsp chopped Dill
- Pinch of Smoked Paprika
- Salt and Pepper, to taste

PREPARATION:

1. Preheat and grease the sandwich maker.

2. Whisk the eggs and season with salt, pepper, garlic powder, and paprika.

3. Stir in the cream cheese, parsley, and cilantro.

4. When the green light appears, pour half of the eggs into the bottom ring of the unit.

5. Top with the shredded cheddar and dill.

6. Lower the top ring and cooking plate, and

---

pour the remaining eggs inside.

7. Close the unit and let cook for 4 to 5 minutes.

8. Rotate the handle clockwise and transfer to a plate.

9. Serve as desired and enjoy!

★ Serving Suggestion:Serve with a side of fresh fruit or a slice of whole grain toast.

★ Variation Tip:Add some sautéed mushrooms or diced bell peppers to the omelet for extra flavor and nutrition.

 **NUTRITION FACTS:**

Calories 290 | Total Fats 22g | Carbs 1.8g | Protein 20.5g | Fiber 0.1g

CHOCOLATE CHIP WAFFLE SANDWICH

 PREPARATION TIME: 5 MINUTES  COOKING TIME: 5 MINUTES SERVINGS: 1

INGREDIENTS

- 2 small frozen waffles
- 1 Tbsp. cream cheese
- 1 Tbsp. mini chocolate chips
- 1 Tbsp. milk
- 1 egg
- Sea salt and pepper

PREPARATION:

1. Spread cream cheese on both waffles. Place one, with the cream cheese side facing up, into the bottom ring of the breakfast sandwich maker. Place the chocolate chips on top.

2. In a small bowl, whisk together the milk, egg, sea salt, and pepper.

3. Lower the cooking plate and top ring. Pour the egg mixture into the egg plate. Place the other waffle on top.

4. Close the cover and cook for 4 to 5 minutes or until the egg is cooked through.

5. Gently slide the egg plate out. Remove the sandwich with a rubber spatula and enjoy!

★ Serving Suggestion: Serve with a side of fresh fruit.

★ Variation Tip: Add some sliced bananas or strawberries to the sandwich for extra flavor and nutrition.

 **NUTRITION FACTS:**

Calories: 450 | Total Fat: 20g | Saturated Fat: 10g | Trans Fat: 0g Cholesterol: 180mg | Sodium: 350mg | Total Carbohydrate: 50g Dietary Fiber: 2g | Sugars: 15g | Protein: 15g

CARAMEL CASHEW WAFFLE SANDWICH

PREPARATION TIME: 5 MINUTES | COOKING TIME: 3 MINUTES | SERVINGS: 1

INGREDIENTS

- 2 small round waffles (store bought or homemade)
- 1 Tbsp. store bought caramel sauce
- 2 Tbsp. finely chopped cashews
- 2 strips bacon
- 1 egg

PREPARATION:

1. Spread caramel sauce on both waffles. Place one waffle into the bottom ring of the breakfast sandwich maker, with the caramel side facing up. Sprinkle the cashews on top, then add the bacon.

2. Lower the cooking plate and top ring. Crack an egg into the egg plate and pierce to break the yolk. Place the other waffle on top.

3. Close the cover and cook for 4 to 5 minutes or until the egg is cooked through.

4. Gently slide the egg plate out and remove the sandwich with a rubber spatula. Slice the sandwich in half.

★ Serving Suggestion: Serve with a glass of cold milk.

★ Variation Tip: Replace the bacon with sausage for a different flavor.

 **NUTRITION FACTS:**

Calories: 650 | Total Fat: 40g | Saturated Fat: 15g | Trans Fat: 0g | Cholesterol: 200mg | Sodium: 700mg | Total Carbohydrate: 55g | Dietary Fiber: 3g| Sugars: 25g| Protein: 20g

OLIVE AND CHEESE SNACK

PREPARATION TIME: 5 MINUTES | COOKING TIME: 3 MINUTES | SERVINGS: 1

INGREDIENTS

- 1 Bread Slice
- 1 ounce Shredded Cheese
- 1 Basil Leaf, chopped
- 2 Kalamata Olives, diced

PREPARATION:

1. Grease the unit and preheat it until the green light appears.

2. Cut the bread slice to fit inside the unit, and place it on the bottom ring.

3. Top with the diced olives, chopped basil, and shredded cheese.

4. Close the lid and cook for 3 minutes.

5. Rotate clockwise and open carefully.

6. Transfer with a non-metal spatula and enjoy!

★ Serving Suggestion: Serve with a side of fresh tomatoes.

★ Variation Tip: Add some slices of cucumber for added crunch.

 **NUTRITION FACTS:**

Calories 205 | Total Fats 12.7g | Carbs 15g | Protein 10g | Fiber 2.1g

ENGLISH MUFFIN SANDWICH

PREPARATION TIME: 5 MINUTES | COOKING TIME: 5 MINUTES | SERVINGS: 1

INGREDIENTS

- 1 slice Cheese
- 1 English Muffin
- 1 slice Canadian Bacon
- 1 Egg, scrambled

PREPARATION:

1. Preheat and grease the sandwich maker.
2. Cut the English muffin in half and place one half with the split-side facing up into the bottom ring.
3. Top with the bacon and cheese.
4. Now, lower the cooking plate and add the scrambled egg inside.
5. Close and let cook for 4 – 5 minutes.
6. Slide clockwise to open using mittens.
7. Remove the sandwich carefully and transfer to a plate.
8. Serve and enjoy!

★ Serving Suggestion: Serve with a side of fresh fruit.

★ Variation Tip: Add some sliced tomatoes or avocado for extra flavor and nutrients.

NUTRITION FACTS:

Calories 357 | Total Fats 17g| Carbs 26g | Protein 24g | Fiber 2g

VANILLA MINI CAKE

PREPARATION TIME: 15 MINUTES | COOKING TIME: 5 MINUTES | SERVINGS: 1

INGREDIENTS

- 1 egg
- 3 tablespoons sugar
- 2 tablespoons milk
- ¼ cup cooking oil/butter
- ½ teaspoon vanilla essence
- ½ cup all-purpose flour/ maida
- ½ teaspoon baking powder

PREPARATION:

1. Add egg and sugar in a bowl and whisk until mixture changes color and fluff up.
2. Now add milk, vanilla essence and oil in the egg mixture and whisk again to combine everything.
3. Add in all-purpose flour, baking powder and fold everything well with a spatula.
4. Preheat your Hamilton Beach Breakfast Sandwich Maker.
5. Lift the top cover, ring, and cooking plate.
6. Now lower the cooking plate and top rings then pour in the prepared batter
7. Cover the top hood, and let the sandwich cook for 5 minutes.
8. When finished cooking, rotate the handle of the cooking plate clockwise until it stops.
9. Lift the hood, the rings and transfer the sandwich to a plate.

★ Serving Suggestion: Serve the sandwich with coleslaw and your favorite sauce on the side.

★ Variation Tip:You can add a drizzle of lemon juice on top of the filling as well.

NUTRITION FACTS:

Calories 192 | Fat 9.3g |Sodium 133mg | Carbs 27.1g | Fiber 1.4g | Sugar 19g | Protein 3.2g

PIZZA SANDWICH

INGREDIENTS

- 2 Bread slices, sourdough
- Butter
- 4 – 5 Chicken strips (you can use pre-cooked)
- 1 tbsp. Marinara sauce
- 8 slices Pepperoni
- 2 slices Cheese, Mozzarella
- ½ tbsp. Parmesan cheese, grated

PREPARATION:

1. Preheat the sandwich maker.
2. Spread butter on each bread slice.
3. On the side without butter, layer the ingredients: place the mozzarella cheese first, followed by the pepperoni slices, then add the marinara sauce, chicken strips, and sprinkle the Parmesan cheese.
4. Top with the other slice of bread, making sure the butter side is facing up.
5. Cook in the sandwich maker for approximately 5 minutes.
6. Serve and enjoy!

★ Serving Suggestion: Serve with a side of garlic breadsticks.

★ Variation Tip: Replace the chicken strips with cooked sausage for a different flavor.

NUTRITION FACTS:

Calories: 550 | Total Fat: 30g | Saturated Fat: 12g | Trans Fat: 0g | Cholesterol: 80mg | Sodium: 900mg | Total Carbohydrate: 45g | Dietary Fiber: 2g | Sugars: 5g | Protein: 25g

ORANGE DREAM DONUT

INGREDIENTS

- 1 medium glazed donut, sliced in half lengthwise
- Cream cheese
- Orange marmalade
- 1 tsp. orange zest
- 1 egg
- Sea salt and pepper

PREPARATION:

1. Spread cream cheese and orange marmalade on both donut halves. Place one half into the bottom ring of the breakfast sandwich maker, with the jam side facing up. Sprinkle with orange zest.
2. Lower the cooking plate and top ring. Crack an egg into the egg plate and pierce to break the yolk. Sprinkle with sea salt and pepper. Place the other donut half on top.
3. Close the cover and cook for 4 to 5 minutes or until the egg is cooked through.
4. Gently slide the egg plate out and remove the donut with a rubber spatula.

★ Serving Suggestion: Serve with a cup of freshly squeezed orange juice.
★ Variation Tip: Add a slice of fresh orange to the filling for an extra citrus burst.

NUTRITION FACTS:

Calories: 450 | Total Fat: 20g | Saturated Fat: 10g| Trans Fat: 0g | Cholesterol: 180mg | Sodium: 350mg | Total Carbohydrate: 55g | Dietary Fiber: 2g | Sugars: 30g | Protein: 12g

STRAWBERRY AND HAZELNUT BAGEL SANDWICH

INGREDIENTS

- ½ Bagel
- 1 tbsp Nutella
- 4 Strawberries, sliced
- 1 tsp chopped Hazelnuts

PREPARATION:

1. Preheat the Hamilton Beach Breakfast Sandwich Maker until the green light appears. Spray it with some cooking spray.

2. Spread the Nutella evenly over the bagel.

3. Place the bagel on the bottom ring, with the cut-side facing up.

4. Arrange the sliced strawberries on top and sprinkle with the chopped hazelnuts.

5. Close the lid and cook for 3 minutes.

6. Rotate the handle clockwise to open.

7. Serve and enjoy!

★ Serving Suggestion: Serve with a cup of hot chocolate.

★ Variation Tip: Replace the strawberries with blueberries for a different flavor.

NUTRITION FACTS:

Calories 220 | Total Fats 8g | Carbs 32g | Protein 5.8g | Fiber 2.2g

BLUEBERRY MARSHMALLOW SANDWICH

INGREDIENTS

- 4 slices of sandwich bread
- Butter, salted, at room temperature
- 6 Marshmallows, jumbo size
- ½ cup chocolate chips, white
- ½ cup Blueberries, fresh

PREPARATION:

1. Preheat the sandwich maker.

2. Spread butter on all sides of each slice of bread.

3. Cut each marshmallow into three pieces and place them on a bread slice. Top with the white chocolate chips and then the fresh blueberries. Cover with another bread slice.

4. Carefully place the 2 sandwiches on the sandwich maker and press firmly.

5. Cook for 2 minutes, then flip the sandwiches. Cook for 2 more minutes.

6. Serve as it is or cut each sandwich in half.

7. Enjoy!

★ Serving Suggestion: Serve with a cold glass of milk.

★ Variation Tip: Instead of white chocolate chips, you can use dark chocolate chips for a richer flavor.

 NUTRITION FACTS:

Calories: 350 | Total Fat: 15g | Saturated Fat: 9g | Trans Fat: 0g | Cholesterol: 20mg | Sodium: 250mg | Total Carbohydrate: 50g | Dietary Fiber: 2g | Sugars: 25g | Protein: 5g

CHOCOLATE BANANA CROISSANT

INGREDIENTS

- 1 small croissant, sliced in half

- 1 Tbsp. chocolate hazelnut spread
- 3 – 4 slices of banana
- Shredded coconut

PREPARATION:

1. Spread the chocolate hazelnut spread on the bottom half of the croissant. Place it in the bottom of the breakfast sandwich maker.

2. Arrange the banana slices on top and sprinkle with some shredded coconut.

3. Lower the cooking plate and top ring. Place the other half of the croissant on top and close the sandwich maker lid.

4. Cook for 2 – 3 minutes or until the croissant is warmed through.

5. Carefully remove from the sandwich maker. Enjoy immediately.

★ Serving Suggestion: Serve with a cup of hot coffee.

★ Variation Tip: Add a drizzle of caramel sauce for an extra sweet treat.

 **NUTRITION FACTS:**

Calories: 380 | Total Fat: 20g | Saturated Fat: 10g | Trans Fat: 0g
Cholesterol: 10mg | Sodium: 150mg | Total Carbohydrate: 45g|
Dietary Fiber: 3g| Sugars: 20g| Protein: 5g

HAM, APPLE, AND CHEESE PANINI

(PREPARATION TIME: 15 MINUTES)   (COOKING TIME: 5 MINUTES)   (SERVINGS: 4)

INGREDIENTS

- 8 slices multigrain bread, cut in 4-inch circle
- 2 tablespoons mayonnaise
- 2 tablespoons Dijon mustard
- 4 tablespoons butter softened
- 8 ounces thick-sliced ham pieces

- 1 small apple cored and thinly sliced
- 8-ounce Swiss cheese grated

PREPARATION:

1. Preheat your Hamilton Beach Breakfast Sandwich Maker.

2. Lift the top cover, ring, and cooking plate.

3. Place a bread slice in the sandwich maker and top with ¼thof the mayo, mustard and butter.

4. Now lower the cooking plate and top rings, then add ¼thof the apple, ham and cheese.

5. Add the other circle of the bread on top.

6. Cover the top hood, and let the sandwich cook for 5 minutes.

7. When finished cooking, rotate the handle of the cooking plate clockwise until it stops.

8. Lift the hood, the rings and transfer the sandwich to a plate.

9. Repeat the same steps with remaining ingredients.

★ Serving Suggestion:Serve the sandwich with crispy bacon and your favorite sauce on the side.

★ Variation Tip:Add some additional ground black pepper to the filling.

 **NUTRITION FACTS:**

Calories 229 | Fat 1.9 |Sodium 567mg | Carbs 1.9g | Fiber 0.4g
| Sugar 0.6g | Protein 11.8g

HONEY APPLE PIE PANINI

(PREPARATION TIME: 15 MINUTES)   (COOKING TIME: 5 MINUTES)   (SERVINGS: 4)

INGREDIENTS

- ½ cup mascarpone cheese
- 2 teaspoons honey

- 4 tablespoons (½ stick) butter
- 8 slices cinnamon raisin bread, cut in 4-inch circle
- 1 Granny Smith apple, cored and sliced
- 2 Tablespoons light brown sugar

PREPARATION:

1. Blend mascarpone cheese with honey, sugar, and butter.
2. Preheat your Hamilton Beach Breakfast Sandwich Maker.
3. Lift the top cover, ring, and cooking plate.
4. Place one bread slice in the sandwich maker and top it with ¼ of the cheese mixture.
5. Lower the cooking plate and top rings, then add ¼ of the apples on top.
6. Add the other bread slice on top.
7. Cover the top hood and let the sandwich cook for 5 minutes.
8. When finished cooking, rotate the handle of the cooking plate clockwise until it stops.
9. Lift the hood, the rings, and transfer the sandwich to a plate.
10. Repeat the same steps with the remaining ingredients.

★ Serving Suggestion: Serve the sandwich with your favorite sauce on the side.
★ Variation Tip: You can add a lettuce leaf to the filling as well.

NUTRITION FACTS:

Calories 183 | Fat 15g | Sodium 402mg | Carbs 2.5g | Fiber 0.4g | Sugar 1.1g | Protein 10g

NUTELLA BANANA PANINI

INGREDIENTS

- 4 slices French bread, cut in 4-inch circle
- 6 tablespoons Nutella spread
- 6 tablespoons Marshmallow cream
- 1 large banana, sliced
- 2 - 3 tablespoons butter

PREPARATION:

1. Preheat your Hamilton Beach Breakfast Sandwich Maker.
2. Lift the top cover, ring, and cooking plate.
3. Place one bread slice in the sandwich maker and top it with ½ of the butter, Nutella spread, and Marshmallow cream.
4. Lower the cooking plate and top rings, then add ½ of the banana slices.
5. Add the other bread slice on top.
6. Cover the top hood and let the sandwich cook for 5 minutes.
7. When finished cooking, rotate the handle of the cooking plate clockwise until it stops.
8. Lift the hood, the rings, and transfer the sandwich to a plate.
9. Repeat the same steps with the remaining ingredients.

★ Serving Suggestion: Serve the sandwich with crispy bacon and your favorite sauce on the side.
★ Variation Tip: Add some additional dried herbs to the filling.

NUTRITION FACTS:

Calories 190 | Fat 18g | Sodium 150mg | Carbs 0.6g | Fiber 0.4g | Sugar 0.4g | Protein 7.2g

CINNAMON STRAWBERRY ENGLISH MUFFIN PIES

PREPARATION TIME: 15 MINUTES   **COOKING TIME: 12 MINUTES**   **SERVINGS: 6**

INGREDIENTS

- 6 English muffins, cut in half
- ½ cup sugar
- 3 tablespoons cornstarch
- ½ teaspoon ground cinnamon
- 1 teaspoon lemon zest
- 1 tablespoon fresh lemon juice
- 2 ½ cups fresh strawberries
- A pinch of salt
- 1 egg yolk
- 2 tablespoons of water
- Sugar, for sprinkling

PREPARATION:

1. Mix strawberries with salt, lemon juice, zest, cinnamon, sugar and cornstarch in a saucepan.
2. Stir and cook berries on low heat for 5 – 7 minutes.
3. Allow this berry filling to cool at room temperature.
4. Preheat your Hamilton Beach Breakfast Sandwich Maker until PREHEAT light gets green.
5. Lift the top cover, ring, and cooking plate.
6. Place half of a muffin inside the bottom tray of the sandwich maker.
7. Add a tablespoon of berry filing to its centre.
8. Place the other top half of the muffin on top.
9. Now lower the cooking plate and top rings.

10. Cover the top hood, and let the sandwich cook for 5 minutes.
11. Rotate the handle of the cooking plate clockwise until it stops.
12. Lift the hood, the rings and transfer the sandwich to a plate.
13. Make more berry pies in the same way.

★ Serving Suggestion:Serve the pie with an apple smoothie on the side.
★ Variation Tip:You can add some mascarpone to the filling as well.

 **NUTRITION FACTS:**

Calories 351 | Fat 19g | Sodium 412mg | Carbs 13g | Fiber 0.3g | Sugar 1g | Protein 23g

NUT BUTTER BANANA CHOCOLATE CHIP PANINI

PREPARATION TIME: 15 MINUTES   **COOKING TIME: 5 MINUTES**   **SERVINGS: 1**

INGREDIENTS

- 2 slices whole-grain bread, cut in 4-inch circle
- 2 tablespoons natural peanut or almond butter (no added salt or sugar)
- 10 bittersweet chocolate chips (60% cocoa)
- ½ banana, sliced

PREPARATION:

1. Preheat your Hamilton Beach Breakfast Sandwich Maker.
2. Lift the top cover, ring, and cooking plate.
3.Place one bread slice in the sandwich maker and top it with peanut butter and chocolate chips

4. Now lower the cooking plate and top rings, then add banana.

5. Add the other circle of the bread on top.

6. Cover the top hood, and let the sandwich cook for 5 minutes.

7. When finished cooking, rotate the handle of the cooking plate clockwise until it stops.

8. Lift the hood, the rings and transfer the sandwich to a plate.

★ Serving Suggestion:Serve the sandwich with coleslaw and your favorite sauce on the side.
★ Serving Suggestion:Serve the sandwich with coleslaw and your favorite sauce on the side.

 **NUTRITION FACTS:**

Calories 267 | Fat 12g | Sodium 165mg | Carbs 39g | Fiber 1.4g | Sugar 22g | Protein 3.3g

BRIE STRAWBERRY CHEESE MUFFIN SANDWICH

 PREPARATION TIME: 15 MINUTES

 COOKING TIME: 5 MINUTES

SERVINGS: 1

INGREDIENTS

- 1 ounce brie, rind removed, and sliced
- 1 English muffins, cut in half
- 1 ounce sliced smoked turkey
- 1 fresh basil leaves, sliced
- 2 tablespoons sliced strawberries
- ½ tablespoon pepper jelly
- ½ tablespoon butter, melted

PREPARATION:

1. Preheat your Hamilton Beach Breakfast Sandwich Maker.

2. Lift the top cover, ring, and cooking plate.

3. Place the lower half of the muffin in the sandwich maker and top it with butter and brie.

4. Now lower the cooking plate and top rings, then add turkey and rest of the fillings.

5. Place another muffin half on top.

6. Cover the top hood, and let the sandwich cook for 5 minutes.

7. When finished cooking, rotate the handle of the cooking plate clockwise until it stops.

8. Lift the hood, the rings and transfer the sandwich to a plate.

★ Serving Suggestion:Serve the sandwich with crispy bacon and your favorite sauce on the side.
★ Variation Tip:Add some additional ground black pepper to the filling.

 **NUTRITION FACTS:**

Calories 102 | Fat 7.6g | Sodium 545mg | Carbs 1.5g| Fiber 0.4g | Sugar 0.7g | Protein 7.1g

LEMONY RASPBERRY ENGLISH MUFFIN PIES

 PREPARATION TIME: 15 MINUTES

 COOKING TIME: 12 MINUTES

 SERVINGS: 6

INGREDIENTS

- ½ cup sugar
- 3 tablespoons cornstarch
- ½ teaspoon ground cinnamon
- 1 teaspoon lemon zest
- 6 English muffin
- 1 tablespoon fresh lemon juice
- 2 ½ cups fresh raspberries
- A pinch of salt
- 1 egg yolk
- 2 tablespoons of water

- Sugar, for sprinkling

PREPARATION:

1. Mix raspberries with salt, lemon juice, zest, cinnamon, sugar and cornstarch in a saucepan.

2. Stir and cook berries on low heat for 5 – 7 minutes.

3. Allow this berry filling to cool at room temperature.

4. Preheat your Hamilton Beach Breakfast Sandwich Maker until PREHEAT light gets green.

5. Lift the top cover, ring, and cooking plate.

6. Place half of a muffin inside the bottom tray of the sandwich maker.

7. Add a tablespoon of berry filing to its centre.

8. Place the other top half of the muffin on top.

9. Now lower the cooking plate and top rings.

10. Cover the top hood, and let the sandwich cook for 5 minutes.

11. Rotate the handle of the cooking plate clockwise until it stops.

12. Lift the hood, the rings and transfer the sandwich to a plate.

13. Make more berry pies in the same way.

★ Serving Suggestion:Serve the pie with a banana smoothie on the side.

★ Variation Tip:You can add some extra cream to the filling as well.

 **NUTRITION FACTS:**

Calories 351 | Fat 19g | Sodium 412mg| Carbs 13g| Fiber 0.3g | Sugar 1g | Protein 23g

Conclusion

The Hamilton Beach breakfast sandwich machine has a simple structure, practical components and excellent function. It can satisfy all kinds of dietary preferences, whether it is the meat sandwich favored by ketogenic eaters, the vegetarian sandwich favored by vegetarians, or the nutritious breakfast sandwich desired by health seekers.

The sandwich maker features two pilot lights, a cooking plate, a detachable assembly ring, a lid, and an upper and lower heating plate. It can quickly make sandwiches in less than five minutes, saving time and costs.

The related recipes revolve around sandwiches, which you can use not only to make delicious breakfast sandwiches, but also to prepare lunch, dinner, or snack sandwiches. The simplicity of operation makes it easy for mothers who prepare breakfast for their children in the busy morning, greatly simplifying their lives. In addition, the appliance is durable and easy to carry.

If you find this book helpful to you, please leave a comment and let more people know. Your feedback will be greatly valued and appreciated.

We hope that this book and this sandwich machine will add more convenience and fun to your life, so that you have a better experience in cooking and eating. Enjoy your food journey!

Thank You!

Dear customer:

We are eager to hear your opinions and suggestions about the author of this book. Your feedback is very valuable to us!

Here's the most exciting part! We will also hold a special event. Click the link below to enter our new sweepstakes. Better chance of winning the big prize. This will be your chance to win big. The selected gifts can be screenshot sent to our email to redeem gifts. We hope you can give us some suggestions and comments when sending the pictures of the redeemed gifts. Look forward to our common progress

PLEASE SCAN THE QR CODE
TO ENTER THE LUCKY DRAW

AUTHOR'S EMAIL:
LAIHONGCHUN70@GMAIL.COM

f you don't want to participate in the lucky draw you can also send us valuable comments by scanning the QR code and unlock a large number of recipe tutorials. What's more, you have the opportunity to download 2,000 recipes for free.

https://forms.gle/2RDDh5SnhWQwTLuP7

Author's email: laihongchun70@gmail.com

wish you a happy life!

Made in the USA
Coppell, TX
10 November 2024

39920983R00070